My Life in My Pocket
for High School Students

Dearest Lou Lu's Divine,

May all your dreams continue to come true! Kathy L. Lewis

My Life in My Pocket
for High School Students
(and those who love them)

K. L. Lewis

Waterfront Press

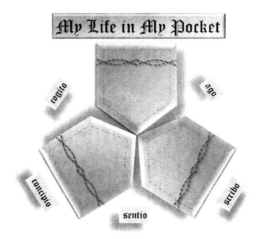

My Life in My Pocket

cogito · ago · concipio · scribo · sentio

Published by Waterfront Publications
ISBN: 978-1-937504-29-8
WP137P

Manufactured in the United States of America, Great Britain, or elsewhere, when purchased outside of North or South America

Book cover and logo design by Bertram A. Lewis, Jr., MD, PhD, MBA, FACS

Produced and distributed for
Waterfront Publications by
Worthy Shorts Publisher Services BackOffice
A CustomWorthy edition

For further information contact
info@worthyshorts.com

To My Daughters

Katherine and Remington

Thank you for being the first students of *My Life in My Pocket.*

It is my hope that I have been the parent you needed
and that I have helped you to have your lives in your pocket.

This book is dedicated to high school students around the world.
Life only gets better as you age—if you plan for it.

Contents

Foreword

As we all evolve and adapt to advances in "connecting to" our families, friends, and the larger world, the challenge to build a healthy and strong sense of self among the young remains a constant. Parents, teachers, and administrators play a key role in this wellness orientation. Each must ask: What can I do to enhance the development of positive attitudes, social skills, and styles of thinking with my student(s)? This refreshingly integrated book provides a treasure trove of exercises, ideas, and complimentary Internet resources to all seeking an answer to that question. Written in a style both appealing and relevant to the high school student, this book is a fun and interactive learning experience.

Angela O. Terry, Ph.D.

Former Associate Vice President,
University of Connecticut

Former State Consultant for School Psychological Services
(Connecticut State Department of Education)

Past President, Friends Board,
Nasher Museum of Art at Duke University

Introduction

*The highest possible stage in moral culture is when we recognize
that we ought to control our thoughts.*

Charles Darwin

This book's sole purpose is to teach you to THINK and to THINK correctly. THINK of this book as a zero to 100-point quiz: you get zero if you
don't write anything in the book and a one-hundred for completing the
book. There are 24 Pockets of Success. Each pocket represents an aspect of
life—a lesson to help you THINK about various situations that many high
school students face. It will show you how to be successful by engaging you
in a conversation with yourself; through the five senses of success: THINK,
Visualize, Feel, Write, and Act, (the sixth sense is to repeat the five senses
of success over and over again). By using the five senses of success you *can*,
and *will*, have your dreams come true if you THINK about them, visualize having them, feel good about them, write them down and act on your
ideas. These thoughts are expressed with everyday words and are often
used without thinking. By thinking about the meaning of these words you
will begin to see how these meanings are reflected in your life. Enjoy this
time that you spend with yourself. It is time well thought!

The only place success comes before work is in the dictionary.

Vince Lombardi
Green Bay Packers Football Coach
The Greatest Football Coach of all Time

Thinking means to form or have in the mind—as an idea or concept.

Cogito Ergo Sum

(I THINK therefore I am).

René Descartes
Philosopher 1596–1650

Forget everything you've heard or thought in the past. Thinking is the most important thing in the world, next to being alive, of course. But can you really live without thinking? Many do, but by not thinking, these individuals are not minding the gap between the life they have and the life they want. They are like bumper cars at a carnival responding only to what bumps into them, letting the trajectory of these bumps determine where they go in life. Thinking will both solve all your problems and help you to avoid them. Thinking actually shapes the world around you. Thinking is the difference between success and failure. Thinking is the one thing we do more than breathing.

The only thing working harder than your mind is your heart. You have about 60,000 thoughts each day; your heart beats about 72 beats per minute—4,320 beats per hour—103,680 beats per day. Your mind works about half as much as your heart. You don't often notice your heart beating, but your thoughts can be all-consuming, especially if they're negative. Thinking can cure a sad life or cause a happy one. Your life, thus far, is the result of your Thinking. Your future will be the result of your thinking. The only thing you can absolutely count on is that you will get what you spend most of your time thinking about. Your mind is an exciting world; in many ways the most exciting adventure in the universe. You should enjoy your thinking. You will find all your hopes and dreams close at hand, not in your heart, but in your mind.

A word is dead

When it is said,

Some say.

I say it just

Begins to live

That day

Emily Dickinson

A **word** is a brief expression; a remark.

Words are powerful. They can heal, harm, hurt, bring joy, cause madness, indicate schizophrenia, ruin self-esteem, cause tears, heighten anxiety, initiate action and, according to the author, Mike Dooley, turn into things. Our language, our wonderful way of communicating to others, and ourselves, isn't just an exchange of pleasantries or intense debate; it is the manner in which we accomplish things. Words spoken aloud have the force of hurricane winds moving ideas from one ear to another via our thoughts—TV, radio, Facebook, YouTube, MySpace, music, pain, and spoken words. All media forms exist because of words.

Words spoken to ourselves, via our thoughts, are omnipotent in that they inspire or degrade. These thoughts, these words, are all-powerful because they either feed our well-being or they steam through us in destruction. That's why each chapter of this book is titled with a single word. Each chapter describes words that are part of our daily well-being and/or our destruction. Many sayings about words are found in The Bible and in everyday children's' language:

"In the beginning was the word, and the word was with God, and the word was God." John 1, verse 1.

Here, the word is a being, a living thing. Words happen and occur. They create and destroy. You must have certain words *"in the pocket,"* in your control, like anger, fear, worry, guilt, and shame. You must also have *"in the pocket"* words like goals, hope, money, and dating. Other sayings about words are:

"Sticks and stones may break my bones but words will never hurt me."

This saying is often used by children, but once we become adults it changes to, *"sticks and stones may break my bones but **words last forever**."* As we mature, we come to recognize the power of words.

More Examples

And God said, "Let there be light," and there was light. Genesis 1, verse 3.

This quote is an example of the power of words. By simply stating something the words *become* something. It's as simple as this; simply say what you want to get what you want.

"Your wish is my command." Whatever you wish will come true.

"Be careful what you wish for." Be careful about your wishes because "words turn into things."

And the <u>word</u> *universe?* This means all created things and phenomena are viewed as constituting one system, a whole—described loosely as *one word*.

Over the next few years you will use many words and make several of the most important decisions of your life: whether or not to have sex, what type of friends to have, how well to perform in school, etc. This book will help you consider these things, but you will have to do some dreaming and some thinking, beginning with answers to a few important questions: What do you want most in the world? What do you want more than anything? What makes you happiest? You should have dreams that stretch far— the next year, five years, twenty years, fifty years; some so high that you may never reach them.

You are now likely thinking "I don't know what I want most in the world." You do know, you just haven't allowed yourself to want it. Wanting what you want just takes a little practice. It is a correct form of thinking. You know what you want, but you're just unaware of the importance of this knowledge.

Here is *my* answer: In addition to the obvious things: peace, good health, love, joy, etc., I want lots of money for myself and lots of money to give away. That is what *I* want most in the world. Your answers should be relatively simple so they can readily be used to replace any negative thoughts or doubts you might have about your goals. Of course, we all want world peace, to end hunger and poverty; but do you see how what I want most in the world covers these things? However, be careful because what you want most in the world need not benefit anyone but you. Sounds selfish? Of course, but if you are selfless then you can't help yourself; by helping yourself you invariably help others. Gandhi said it best, "whatever you do in life will be insignificant, but do it anyway because if *you* don't, no one else will."

Thinking about the rest of your life even before completing high school can seem like an arduous task, but after a few minutes you will begin to have fun. There is nothing more wonderful than your imagination. As you THINK about your future, imagine all the wonderful experiences you want to have; all the wonderful places you want to go. **Life can be, and should be, spent in the wonders of your dreams and in the reality of them coming true.**

The objective of life is development. You must learn and grow as you live. The way to learn and grow throughout life is to continually set and achieve the goals. The space between setting a goal and achieving it is where conflict dwells. In this space, while undergoing conflict, confidence develops. Setting and achieving goals builds confidence. Being a confident person is an improvement upon your world and the world you are in.

Who is the most important and confident person in the world (to you)?

_____

Whenever I ask this question in seminars, I get a variety of answers: Mom, God, Dad, etc., but the real answer should and must be—*I* **am!** Now answer the question again, **who is the most important and confident person in the world (to you)?** _____. You must be the most important person to you; if what you want most in the world seems only to benefit you initially, that is the perfect answer, because viewing something that appears to benefit only yourself as something bad is a myth.

Everything we want that is in the realm of something good benefits others. If you do things that benefit yourself it makes you a better person and thereby benefits others. If you do not spend a lot of time worrying about problems and are, instead, actually enjoying the things you want, you are becoming a better person. So getting what one wants in life makes us better people.

What do you want most in the world? (Remember—all answers receive a grade of "A")

Think of the biggest, baddest goal for yourself. Write the first thing that comes to mind.

_____

_____

You can Have, Do, or Be anything. *Any-thing!!!*

What do you want to have?

_____

_____

What do you want to do?

_____

_____

What do you want to be?

_____

_____

To love oneself is the beginning of a lifelong romance.

Oscar Wilde

How Goals Can Suddenly Appear

When I was about 19 years old I wrote on my list of goals that I wanted a black belt in karate. When I was 23, it appeared. I was working in a government office where I met an older guy. He was impressive, and when he walked away someone mentioned that he was a fourth degree black belt. It turned out that my university offered a free class for students and alumni. So I took karate for eight years, four or more nights a week, at no cost except for advancement tests. There was nothing that was going to stop me.

During the first six months, I swore, every night, that if I finished the class I would never return. It was the hardest exercise I'd ever done in my life. It was miserable, and I wanted to quit, but I couldn't. Somehow, each night I would be back in class swearing I would never return. Finally, after about six months, I began to enjoy the class. I look back now and I know that all I just said is true because I wrote it down; it had a life of its own.

Write down more about what you want to do with your life. Don't stop with age 20 or 25. What about age 30, 50, 70, 90? Include things like running a marathon or winning a Nobel Prize, or becoming an astronaut, or starting a business. Dream Big! Don't be afraid of your dreams; write down what you want. Your current circumstances are irrelevant. Where you are today does not determine where you will be tomorrow. What determines your tomorrow is what you THINK about today.

Write down what you're thinking about for your future. Be Bold!

_____

_____

_____

_____

_____

_____

_____

_____

_____

Now, was that so bad? Look at what you wrote; go on, look at it! Realize that you've already achieved 80% of what you have written down. Simply by writing things down gives them an 80% chance of happening. Just writing things down gives them life and a mind of their own. Things often happen in spite of our reluctance, just as was the case of my karate goal.

What you THINK, feel, and do secretly is sooner or later shouted from the housetops either as failure or success in your life.

Catherine Ponder
Author of _The Dynamic Laws of Prosperity_

Many of you believe that what you really feel and THINK is a secret. You THINK these feelings and thoughts are hidden from the world, but your thoughts, feelings, and actions are revealed to the world through the life you lead. You know who the successful people are by the way they look and behave. You also know the unsuccessful people by the way _they_ look and behave. Your drug-using classmates often sleep in class and do not pay attention (if they come to school at all), while successful students are enthusiastic and attentive to their studies. Nothing is hidden for long. To be a success in high school, and thus have a successful beginning in life, there are three simple, but not easy, things you need to do:

3 Keys To A Successful Beginning

1. **Keep a clear mind. (Don't do drugs or drink alcohol.)**

2. **Treat your body well. (Don't have sex while in high school.)**

3. **Get "A"s and "B"s. (Do your best possible academic work and never settle for "C"s or "D"s.)**

Now, for you extremely intelligent, but misguided students who *will* use drugs, *will* have sex, and *won't* do your best work in school, seriously THINK about why you do these things.

Why do you choose to do these harmful things?

_____

_____

_____

_____

If you don't do harmful things to yourself, write why you choose not to.

_____

_____

_____

_____

There is a reason—and I'm sure you thought of it instantly. If you didn't, once you start thinking about your life, your life will change.

Why Do Some Kids Use Drugs?

My cousins and neighborhood-friends offered me drugs. I said, "No." They said, "What? Do you think you're too good for us?" I said, "Yes." This exchange occurred a few more times, but I stood fast and in the end I chose not to drink and not to use drugs. The peer pressure was short-lived so don't worry about not fitting in. Your peers will move on quickly from offering drugs if you're firm and unwavering in saying "No." I won the respect of my cousins and neighbors. I remained part of the group, but they stopped offering me drugs and alcohol. They wanted me to go out with them because I could be the designated driver and I became their moderator of sobriety." This example is not to say that I condone drinking as long as it's not me. Drinking is for adults only, after age 21. This story demonstrates that saying "no" to your peers does not necessarily mean that you will lose that group of friends. Although the type of people you spend time with should fit into the goals you have set. Just say **"no"** to drugs and you will gain respect.

> *You are the average of the five people you spend the most time with.*
>
> Jim Rohn
> *Self-made millionaire and successful author*

When I was in ninth grade, I wrote an essay about attending parties and my feeling that it was a waste of time. My English teacher, Ms. Davis, told me that I would have plenty of time to attend parties when I became an adult. She said I should follow my heart and stay home with my books. Her comment was so validating! I've never forgotten it. She told me that it was perfectly acceptable to have a goal to be successful in school. You must follow your gut. If something doesn't feel right, don't do it. You're the only one who can be the true judge of that. Listen to the positive things you tell yourself.

Drinking and using drugs adds to the *nec spe nec metu* (without hope, without fear) concept that often permeates teenage thinking. Drug use causes you to lose your inhibitions and to stop thinking. All you are doing while using drugs is feeling, not thinking. The use of drugs is an escape from living. In middle school or high school, where most students are first exposed to drugs, look at the people who are offering you drugs or are using drugs. Are these people you want to be like? If your answer is anything but "no," please get help before you even begin to THINK of using drugs. Tell your parents, your school counselor, or a close family friend. Face the fear of talking about this. Initiate a pre-intervention. Stop the flow of negative thoughts. Visit www.MyLifeinMyPocket.com and click on the book series, >HighSchool>Intro

What's your story? What are your thoughts about school? Do those thoughts detract from, or contribute to, your success?

_____

_____

_____

_____

Remember the dreams for your life that you wrote of earlier; your future? How will you deal with drugs now? What will you say the next time someone offers you drugs or alcohol? Write your "just say no" script.

_____

_____

_____

Join the conversation #pocketintroduction

The mind is its own place, and in itself

Can make a Heav'n of Hell, a Hell of Heav'n.

Milton

The 24
Pockets of Success

POCKET #1

Goals

#pocket1goals

You want to set a goal that is big enough that in the process of achieving it you become someone worth becoming.

Jim Rohn
Business Philosopher

Goals are the purpose toward which endeavors are directed.

My grandmother told me that I could be anything I wanted to be when I grew up. She gave me my first adult book, *The Dynamic Laws of Prosperity*, by Catherine Ponder, when I was 14 years old. I devoured it and began thinking about my goals and dreams. By setting goals your life will take on a life of its own and it will unfold right before your eyes.

List some of the people you admire. Thinking about how others achieve success will inspire you to do the same. I like Mark Zuckerberg. I like the way he completely changed the way we entertain ourselves.

_____

_____

_____

_____

_____

_____

_____

Believing in what you want and what you like to do is important. Treasure the things you like. These things may be very different from the things your parents, friends, or siblings enjoy. You can have a wonderful idea about how to do something, but you dismiss it even before you try because it lacks someone's approval.

Write down all your ideas in a small book you keep with you at all times (or on your IPad or smartphone). You're at an age where ideas will flood your mind. Keep a log of them. These ideas are the foundation for success. These ideas are examples of correct thinking. Ideas are the portals through which success filters.

Some people think that living in clean government housing, and maybe not working, or living a mediocre life, is the easy path; that committing to education through study is the hard path. They're wrong! Failing to follow your dreams and not reach your potential is the path to conformity and mediocrity—the easy path. Choosing what looks like the easy path leads to under-achievement.

This is peer pressure. It is others wanting you to do what they do. As you attempt to succeed there will be those who act like "crabs in a bucket." When one crab climbs to the top, the others pull it down by also trying to get to the top and causing everyone to fail. This is also an example of "Group-THINK," conforming to the ideas of the wrong group of people around you; in your neighborhoods and schools they are often those having negative or mediocre goals. "Group-THINK" is an incorrect way of thinking. If you simply conform to the way the masses THINK then you are conforming to the way the masses live, and you will live like that. THINK a particular way because it is in line with the life you have decided live. Live the life you want to, not a life of conformity. Deciding to be like everyone else simply because everyone else does a particular thing is a most dangerously incorrect way to THINK; dangerous because it robs you of the life you want because it appears like it is the correct thing to do—because everyone else is doing it.

You will have your life *"in your pocket"* by thinking correctly about your goals and believing in your unique ideas. Know what you want and where you're going. The way to know where you are going is to THINK about it, visualize what you want, feel good about it, write it down, and act upon your ideas; these are the Five Senses of Success: THINK, Visualize, Feel, Write and Act!

Where are you going? What do you want? THINK, Visualize, Feel, Write, and then Act. List them all below:

_____

_____

_____

_____

_____

_____

_____

_____

Wanting money and nice things, the best things in life is not the problem. This is not a character flaw. What you must do is THINK positively about money. Friends, family, your parents, they may tell you that money is the root of all evil. This is an often misquoted biblical saying. The actual quote from _The Journey,_ the New International Version of the Bible, comes from 1 Timothy 6, verse 10 which says, "For the love of money is a root of all kinds of evil." The lack of money and other resources is often the catalyst for inaction and failure. You believe you can't do a particular thing because of something you lack, so you never try.

How many hopes and dreams have you abandoned in your life because of a lack of money, or support, or some other form of lack? Write them down.

_____

_____

_____

_____

_____

_____

_____

Did you fail to, for example:

try out for a sport?

join the cheer-leading squad?

make new friends outside of your current circle?

Abandoning dreams is so easy to do that you often will do it without even noticing. *Easy* doesn't even begin to really describe it properly. Giving up your goals is a very simple process. You simply don't act upon your ideas. Not acting is easy because you allow yourself to be distracted by the everyday worries of your life and fail to achieve your goals which represent your future life—a priority—by getting swept up in the winds of "busyness." Don't let these winds swirl you into chaos and distract you from the life you want. Make your goals your number one priority.

How much time will you devote each day to reach your goals through thinking, visualizing, feeling, writing, and taking action? How will you hold yourself accountable to your commitment to achieving these goals? You should commit to doing at least three things each day that will move you toward your goals. What will you do each day to move closer to your goals? Write as many as you can THINK of here, then choose three each day and implement the sixth sense of success by repeating your actions as you THINK of more to add:

_____

_____

_____

_____

_____

_____

_____

_____

_____

_____

Read your goals four times a day. Read them as soon as you wake up and just before you go to sleep as well as two more times during the day—especially when you feel fear, worry or doubt.

A fear of realizing your goal is an irrational feeling. Because you feel fear you give up the best pieces of your life. Your hopes and dreams come from an inner voice. I call this voice the gap minder. Goals help to close the gap between the life you want and the life you have. Victor Hugo said, *"An invasion of armies can be resisted but not an idea whose time has come."* Your hopes and dreams are ideas whose time has come. Once the moment you THINK of them is past, most of the hard work is done. You only have to carry out an action to wait for the next step to appear. This process should be fun and easy. If you find it too difficult then this may not be the right path. Act on the thoughts that feel right. Where you are in your life and where you will be in the future is a result of your thoughts. Your imagination creates your life. Or the absence of imagination will do the reverse, not instantly like an instant message but eventually, like an Internet virus, by thinking one negative thought after another.

What are some of your personal goals? Just write down whatever comes to mind. I wrote down "get a black belt" and it gained a life of its own.

_____

_____

_____

_____

_____

_____

_____

_____

_____

_____

_____

THINK about people in your life that you genuinely like, admire, and get along with. List the qualities that attracted you to them and those that sustain your interest.

_____

_____

_____

_____

What are the qualities of your perfect friend?

_____

_____

_____

_____

Now, dream big. What are the qualities of the perfect boyfriend or girlfriend? Don't settle for anything less than what you want simply because they don't live in your neighborhood or go to your school. Write down their physical, emotional, and educational attributes. Be specific.

_____

_____

_____

_____

_____

_____

_____

_____

_____

_____

Winning isn't everything, but the will to win is everything.

Vince Lombardi
Legendary Football Coach

Qualities You Should Have

Look your best all the time. Do your best in all things. Whenever I had exams I would wear my best outfit. Whenever I had a job interview I would buy a new suit or dress. I'd put on a piece of my favorite jewelry; fix my hair in a special way. People respect that. People remember it. Even when you wear sweats, look your best. Do that *little something extra* to make it pop. You may slough around the house, but don't leave the house looking a mess. Young men should wear clean t-shirts and jeans. It is really insignificant what you wear, just be sure it represents you and is cleaned and pressed. You should always dress in a manner that suits you. Russell Simmons built an empire while wearing Adidas sportswear.

I love Caroline Herrera, Michael Kors, Ralph Lauren, Burberry, Hugo Boss, Tommy Hilfiger, Calvin Klein, Sean John, Phat Farm and Baby Phat. What's your style? What type of clothes do you like? What designer will you wear? What type of car will you drive? What kind of house will you live in? Write down what you want not what you think you can get. Question everything especially your negative thoughts. It takes courage to follow your dreams. It takes courage to stand up for yourself. On the following pages add pictures from magazines, the Internet or pictures you've taken of the things you like.

Things I Like

Add pictures from magazines, the Internet, or photos you've taken of the things you like and the things you want to have, do, or be.

Things I Like

Add pictures from magazines, the Internet, or photos you've taken of the things you like and the things you want to have, do, or be.

Things I Like

Add pictures from magazines, the Internet, or photos you've taken of the things you like and the things you want to have, do, or be.

Things I Like

Add pictures from magazines, the Internet, or photos you've taken of the things you like and the things you want to have, do, or be.

Now, create a personal statement. Your statement should summarize what you want to have, do, and be. Your statement should be one to three sentences and should be written 15 times daily. Your personal statement should always be stated in the present tense. Each time you write your personal statement your belief in the statement will grow. My personal statement is *"I am grateful, I am happy, I am healthy, and I am wealthy."* Also say your statement to yourself during times of fear, worry, anger, guilt, and shame and, especially, during times of joy.

These statements will at first feel like untruths, but you have to lie to yourself so that you start believing in yourself. It is what Alcoholics Anonymous refers to as, "acting as if," acting as if you already are the person you want to be.

_____

_____

_____

_____

_____

_____

_____

_____

_____

Join the conversation #pocket1goals

The major reason for setting a goal is for what it makes of you to accomplish it.

What it makes of you will always be the far greater value than what you get.

Jim Rohn
American speaker and author

POCKET #2

Hope

#pocket2hope

"Hope" is the thing with feathers -

That perches in the soul -

And sings the tune without the words -

And never stops - at all -

And sweetest - in the Gale - is heard -

And sore must be the storm -

That could abash the little Bird

That kept so many warm -

I've heard it in the chillest land -

And on the strangest Sea -

Yet, never, in Extremity,

It asked a crumb - of Me.

Emily Dickinson 1861
Poet

Hope is the feeling that what is wanted will happen.

"Hope is the thing with feathers" as Emily Dickinson's amazing phrase puts it so engagingly in her poem about hope. It never stops. It is always fluttering around inside of you. I had been hoping for something all my life. My hope had just about run its course. For as long as I can remember there was never enough of anything, but, in particular, there was never enough money. My childhood and most of my adult life was spent in the undying hope of having enough and surviving: surviving a childhood that included an alcoholic father; surviving middle school and neighborhood violence; surviving the academic void left in me by attending a poorly funded elementary school and middle school, even though I was a bright student.

Living "without enough" as a child has had lasting effects. The void of not having "enough" was also created by an absence of stimulating experiences. The daily drudgery of walking to school through filth and garbage and returning home through the same filth and garbage combined with a lack of positive experiences, and a general permeation of apathy, this was absolutely contagious. There were times when I wanted so desperately to *not want* a better life. It was so hard to stay focused on school work during my parent's arguments. It was so hard to have peace about school when I knew I would need a dress for the ring dance and coming proms. There were times when I told myself that wanting a different life was some kind of curse, because if these wants were so important then surely it would not be so difficult to stay motivated in pursuit of this better life. I desperately did not want to care, but for some reason, I could not lose hope.

To immunize myself against this apathy I had to constantly hope for a better life. As I walked home I would force myself to imagine walking through a beautiful neighborhood with lots of trees, flowers, and grass. I wanted so desperately to escape, that, before sleep, I spent every night in bed daydreaming about my future. Those nights were so comforting because my dreams seemed so real. I did this without knowing how important visualization was and that I was shaping my future. I hoped *so much* that I forgot to take action. By the time I was an adult, hope had become agony. I hated to hope. I was hopeless. What I wanted was not happening. Hope had turned into disappointment, and the only way to survive disappointment after losing hope is through apathy—the one very thing I thought I had been inoculated from by hoping!

This vicious cycle of hope: hope becoming disappointment, disappointment becoming apathy, and apathy sustaining itself through the absence of emotion. By feeling nothing you will do nothing. I wanted to be numb. I understood why so many easily turn to drugs and alcohol in an attempt to lessen the pain. I wanted to be just like everyone around me—hopeless. Hope had turned into a miserable struggle. The storms of life had devastated my hope, but somehow I could not give up my dream for a better life. I reached out for Emily Dickinson's feather and easily caught hope again.

How do you hold on to that feeling? How do you hold on to hope? You hold on to hope by hoping. How do you regain something that has been lost? You must use what you have lost—hope. This is a strange oxymoron, finding hope with hope but remember, "hope,' is the thing with feathers." It is inside you, but when you no longer feel it "perching in your soul" all you have to do is lift your head and grab it! It is easy as catching a feather. Hope simply floats in the air hoping to be caught and perch in your soul again. Just lift your hand and grab it!

Many of you are filled with anxiety and uncertainty. You are hoping that your life will turn out to be like you imagined, that what you want will happen, but as Benjamin Franklin said, "he that lives upon hope dies fasting." You can hope that things will improve in your life, but if you are not thinking, visualizing, feeling, writing down goals and taking action to meet your goals that's all you will be—just hopeful, just waiting. Hope must be attended by action and because of the work you're doing in this book, your achievements will be stupendous! Although you will experience challenges, I believe that with this book and your ability to coordinate as a team with this book, I anticipate great success and I am hopeful for your academic future and your future in general. Be bold with your hope! Hope for the highest of the highest of the things you want in life. The only thing that hope asks of you is that you hope. Pick the biggest, baddest dream and hope for it, confident that, through your actions, your big dream will rush toward you like a tsunami and flood your life with your fulfilled hopes and dreams—all of them!

What are you hopeful for in the future? Write those hopes here. And, should hope no longer "perch in your soul," how will you make the small effort to reach out and grab it?—because it is as easy as catching a feather. Describe how you will recapture hope.

_____

_____

_____

_____

_____

_____

_____

_____

_____

_____

_____

_____

_____

_____

_____

_____

_____

_____

_____

Join the conversation #pocket2hope

We must accept finite disappointment,
but never lose infinite hope.

Martin Luther King, Jr.
Nobel Prize Winner for Peace

POCKET #3

Disappointment

#pocket3disappointment

The size of your success is measured by the strength of your desire;

*the size of your dream; and how you handle
disappointment along the way.*

Robert Kiyosaki
Author of "Rich Dad, Poor Dad" Series

Disappointment is to fail to fulfill the expectation or hope of.

Disappointment is not something to understand, it is something to overcome. Once you start moving toward your hopes and dreams you may begin to expect praise from others. The more you do something good, the less praise you get for it. You must continue to move toward your goals without the hope of praise. Praise is a pacifier for your ego and should not be taken personally, just as you should not take criticism personally. If your hopes and dreams need approval from others, then the dream is not your dream. Approval from others waters down what you want. The mind can become muddy when in search of approval, causing an inability to see your goals clearly. You must want a thing simply because you want it; not because someone else wants it, or THINKS it is a good idea, or because it pleases someone else. Be mature when thinking about your future. It must be your future; not the silly hopes and dreams that require obtaining approval. Of course we want others to acknowledge what we achieve, but this cannot be the motivation. Your internal praise is all you need! Remember to self-parent. Love yourself and praise yourself. Reward yourself when you behave well. When others do this it will be gravy, not the main course; it will be good, but not necessary. If your thoughts are positive, and you believe in your hopes and dreams, then whatever anyone else has to say will have no effect on you—positive or negative.

Grades

Disappointment is one of the most common feelings people experience and one of the most difficult to overcome. It is rarely discussed seriously. Society views it as "no big deal." But it *is* something difficult to conquer. The sting when an expectation goes unmet can be debilitating. When you let disappointment permeate your mind, you bury your dreams; deeper and deeper beneath each disappointment. There will be times when you feel that you are buried under mounds and mounds of disappointment.

Your belief system is created from your ability to handle disappointment. Recognize the feeling of disappointment and replace it with perseverance. Disappointment is not a loss; it is a signal telling you to focus—focus on what you are trying to accomplish, not the disappointment. One of my biggest disappointments was getting a "C" in college. It was in African-American literature. I remember feeling awful because I had enjoyed the course, and it was brand new, the first time such a course was offered. I had a hard time "getting over" this grade and still cringe a little when I think about it.

That disappointing grade would pop up in my thoughts whenever I found myself struggling with a subject. It was as if the "C" was somehow attached to my DNA and now was a permanent part of my being. I consoled myself with the notion that in the business world "A" students tend to work for the "C" students but a "C" is never a good idea! Always do your best in all things, Only "A's" and "B's" please. Remember you can **have**, **do**, and **be** anything, *ANY-THING!!*

When you experience a flood of disappointment it simply means a flood of good will follow. Floods of disappointment are wonderful "wake-up" calls that provide a cleansing of your character. You must *not* be discouraged by such things in life. Review your goals and move on. Each negative experience is just your good turned inside out. You may THINK it was the result of an unfair or tyrannical teacher, or your parents, or your boyfriend, or your girlfriend, or your best friend. Just stop it! It is nothing but the beginning of success. Failure is the beginning of success because failing is a by-product of moving forward with action; constant, persistent action brings success!

How well will you control your thinking when faced with disappointment? What you THINK is what your life *is* and what your life *will* become. Train yourself to THINK in positive, motivating ways. You've

heard the saying "people get what they deserve"—WRONG! People get what they THINK and what they THINK is what they deserve.

How will you handle future disappointment? THINK, and write many solutions here:

_____

_____

_____

_____

_____

_____

_____

_____

_____

_____

_____

_____

_____

_____

Join the conversation #pocket3disappointment

*Disappointment to a noble soul is
what cold water is to burning metal;*

it strengthens, tempers, intensifies, but never destroys it.

Eliza Tabor
Novelist

POCKET #4

Self-Parenting

The Founding Fathers in their wisdom decided that children were an unnatural strain on parents.

So they provided jails called schools, equipped with tortures called an education.

John Updike
American Writer

Self means the essential person distinct in identity from all other persons.

Parenting is the raising of a child by its parents.

Self-Parenting (as defined by me) is the care of self without regard to a contradictory or dysfunctional environment.

The idea of self-parenting is a tough but very important subject. You must listen to parents while being aware of undue influence that goes against your moral compass. You may not have the same beliefs as your parents. Just because your beliefs are different, this does not mean you are wrong or crazy. Parents are necessary but they are ***not*** sufficient. This means that parents are absolutely necessary, but you must follow *your* conscience and moral compass; a belief of your own making, while continuing to build upon the parenting you received.

Necessary and sufficient means "A" occurs if, and only if, "B" occurs. So, if parental guidance is enough, then it would mean that you would be a good and complete person because your parents raised you properly. It doesn't work out that way. Not all children who are properly raised turn out to be good and complete people; so what does being properly raised mean anyway?

The probability of being a good and complete person is much greater if you receive proper parenting. Being reared properly includes obtaining certain foundational beliefs that help move you toward being a good, complete person. It means feeling loved and cared for; having sufficient food, clothing, and shelter; proper discipline; and encouragement to do well in school. But parents never fail to disappoint; they fail *constantly* while they succeed *mostly*.

Even with good parenting, continue to develop your *own* moral compass. Cultivate your *own* opinion about what is right or wrong. Build on the framework your parents provided by using your *own* mortar. Parents give you the bricks (the building blocks), you must supply the mortar (glue) that are your inner beliefs. "Bad kids" have chosen a different mortar. Often these kids have great parents. Those parents have provided their children with great bricks (building blocks), but the children have chosen a mortar that is socially, legally, and morally unacceptable. By their own choice, their bricks are held together by destructive mortar. They have allowed their friends and their surroundings to dictate who they are. What will you do if your parents are racist or intolerant of people who are different from them? If you discover this failing, will you automatically agree with them, or will you decide to build with a different mortar?

Legally, at a certain age, society expects you to be responsible for your actions. The way in which your parents raised you does not become an issue, unless the law is broken. This implies that some form of self-parenting is necessary as we have learned that not all parenting is good parenting. Live in your imagination if you have no one else to turn to.

Religiously, you may be held to another standard which can also be at odds with your parents' beliefs. Sometimes one may find oneself part of a religion different from one's parents; another form of self-parenting. How can your parents know what they do not know? How do you know what your parents do not know? You figure this out by thinking about the good and complete person you want to be.

Lindsey was 15 years old. She and her older sister were regularly told by their mom that certain bills were due, and they should use *whatever means necessary* to make money to pay these bills. This resulted in that mom's two young daughters sexually selling themselves to earn money for their mom. Mom, in essence, was their pimp. I asked Lindsey, "Why don't you just let the electricity get disconnected?" She said she never thought that was an option. I could see in her face that it had never occurred to her to refuse. Of course, this is an extreme example of a "mom-gone-bad." Lindsey's mother's moral compass was totally out-of-whack. This daughter was in dire need of self-parenting because her parent was horribly misguided and detrimental to her well-being.

That was an awful example, but what if your parents have a more liberal or conservative view than yours? How will you self-parent in those areas that are different from your parents'? THINK about the type of person you want to be and incorporate those characteristics into your behavior. It is important to make your own mortar, wrap yourself in your own fabric of ideals, and build your character accordingly. It is important to believe in yourself especially when you don't.

What areas of your life would you like to grow in that is different from your parents? What areas are the same? A good place to start is with education. You should not permit your parents to be more educated than you. THINK of other things you'd like to be different and write them here:

_____

_____

_____

_____

_____

_____

_____

_____

Join the conversation #pocket4selfparenting

You have to believe in yourself when no one else does.

That's what makes you a winner.

Venus Williams
Professional Tennis Champion

POCKET #5

Negativity

(The Ugly Side of Life)

#pocket5negativity

Every negative event contains within it the seed of an equal or greater benefit.

Napoleon Hill
Author of "THINK and Grow Rich"

Negativity is the quality or condition that results in attacking the positive.

The Five Senses of Negativity: Fear, Worry, Hate, Guilt, and Shame.

The Five Senses of Success: THINK, Visualize, Feel, Write, and Act.

There is a rogue kingdom inside of you. The King is Fear and the Queen is Anger. **In fact, The Queen, Anger, is so powerful that I have given her a separate pocket, #6.** Other members of the court are Worry, Hate, Guilt, and Shame. This inner kingdom is what keeps you from getting what you want. You must form a coup d'état and reclaim your inner world. You worry about your problems, fear that you cannot solve them, and are ashamed because you have them. Everyone has problems. *Everyone!* And FEAR is the fertilizer for problems. Let's begin with one's most popular emotion— The King, Fear.

Fear is an unpleasant, often strong emotion caused by the expectation for or the awareness of danger. As the author Joyce Meyers states:

F - False

E - Evidence

A - Appearing

R - Real

The awareness of danger is one thing, but perceiving of something as dangerous when it is not is quite easy to do; we all experience this type of fear at various times in our lives. You THINK, just because your negative thoughts have great intensity, that they are meaningful. But this is a trick; it is a coup, an attack from the kingdom within you. Negative thinking derives from the five senses of negativity: fear, worry, hate, guilt, and shame while positive thinking comes from the five senses of success: THINK, visualize, feel, write, and act. Negative thinking also comes from self-hatred, all of which measures the bulk of fear. Some examples of fear as self-hatred:

- "don't even try"

- "why bother?"

- "whatever!"

- "I can't"

- "you'll never make it"

- "who do you THINK you are?"— (others enjoy asking you this also)

- "you don't deserve it"

- "you suck"

Ad infinitum, Ad nauseam (Latin for "without end or limit and to a sickening degree") .

To overcome fear, all you have to do is one thing— don't let it stop you! Fear and excitement have the same effect physically. Every time you feel fear, THINK of it as a request to do what you fear, unless it is genuinely dangerous.

You must do the thing you fear. Mark Victor Hansen, author of *One Minute Millionaire*, states that you must do FTFs first; do your "feared things first." The more you move through the fear, the less you will notice it. I am sure I feel fear, but I no longer notice it. I am too busy thinking about my actions; how to move forward. When you feel fear, use that fear as the fuel for doing your best in a new situation; consider it the energy required to take action. Often the feeling of fear is driven by your negative thoughts and creates fear in you that is unnecessary. For example, a major fear on the road to success is the fear of alienating friends and family members as you become successful. Do you have this fear? What other fears do you have? How do these fears hold you back in life? How are they irrational? How will you handle your emotions the next time you feel fear?

Join the conversation #pocket5fear

In order to learn the important lessons in life one must each day surmount a fear.

Ralph Waldo Emerson

Worry is to make anxious or upset.

Worry is the greatest instigator of negative thinking. When you worry you beat yourself up by focusing on everything that is wrong with a person, place, or thing. There is always something wrong! Never deny the fact that bad things happen; simply decide that you will change your thinking about the bad things. Ninety percent of what you worry about never happens and the remaining ten percent doesn't happen the way you imagined it would.

You can become consumed with worry with no relief in sight. You worry about appearing silly, or doing something embarrassing, so you decide to not do anything! As a result of worry, some people make a decision deep inside themselves that life is not worth living. I'm not talking about suicide. I'm referring to the time you failed to try out for a team, failed to attend a social engagement, failed to accept an invitation to lunch or dinner, failed to ask a teacher for help. This is a life unlived. All it takes to do any of those things is a little courage. That courage is a small part of the process. You only need a bit of courage to get into the car and go there. Once it's done the worry goes away. Even if you get there and end up not liking it, that's unimportant. The doing of the thing is only a byproduct, a part of the process; the success is in taking the step!

People often say, "I don't have any money, and I worry about it all the time." Worry is a form of fear, in this case the fear of being poor. If you constantly THINK about not having enough you will never fail at not having enough!

If you have the constant thought that "no one likes me," which creates an unlikable personality, this *will* create the belief that "no one likes me." And, in fact, no one *will* like you. This, in turn, causes a lack of friends which creates a *reality* that "no one likes me." This is a "rut," (a worry loop). If you fail to make a conscious effort to interrupt the worry loop, you can stay in this loop for your entire life.

Worry makes it easy to "stop living" (to discontinue following your dreams). It is too easy to "get by" in life. You give up your hopes and dreams and merely exist when responding to situations rather than planning your life. It takes courage to live the life you want. Courage is not some big, overwhelming thing that requires using all your energy to muster up action. Courage is simply believing in yourself and taking a step—a single step. Take one step toward your goal. That is all you need to do! Each step grows easier as you go along. Stop worrying about your problems; instead, take action to solve them. They will not go away on their own, so face them immediately and watch your life change in a most positive and remarkable way! What will you do the next time you feel worry? Will you replace this negative emotion with a positive view of your hopes and dreams? What are you currently worried about? How can you change this worry into a positive agent in your life?

I have lived a long life and had many troubles,

most of which never happened.

Mark Twain
American Author

List three of your most pressing problems, then write the outcome you desire for each. List the steps you will take to reach the desired outcome. Then take that action and your problems will be solved; if not fully solved, they will forever be altered in a positive way.

_____

_____

_____

_____

_____

_____

_____

_____

_____

_____

_____

_____

_____

_____

_____

_____

_____

_____

_____

_____

_____

As we focus and control our thoughts,

we can change our beliefs and ultimately the condition of our lives.

Iyanla Vanzant
Inspirational Speaker and Author

If you do as the above quote suggests, success is not just possible. By following through with action, it becomes inevitable. This works even if you cannot believe it. Even though you might find Ms.Vanzant's quote incredulous, begin controlling your thoughts. This is one of the few times that belief is not necessary for success. You have to lie to yourself to begin to believe in yourself. Tell yourself that everything does go your way; say to yourself, "I am successful!" Change the negative thoughts you have about yourself to positive statements. Become self-aware. Be vigilant about controlling your mind, your body, and your emotions. Refuse to let a negative kingdom run amok inside of you. Use introspection to conquer that kingdom because, when thinking negatively, you can be completely unaware of it.

For example, I took the class in college, "Sociology of Children." After taking an exam that I was completely unprepared for, I found myself in a state of absolute fear. My heart pounded like a throbbing headache when my professor returned the exam. She looked at me with a strange expression on her face that I perceived to mean that I had done terribly on the test. My inner kingdom was running wild with negative thoughts and feelings. Even though my professor did not have a look of disappointment on her face it *was* an unusual look. I thought that that look was warning me that I had failed miserably.

When taking the test, I had felt completely and totally unprepared. Each question brought with it debilitating doubt, a feeling I was unaccustomed to experiencing while taking tests, so the doubt created panic and the panic made me believe that I was going to fail even though I had only answered three questions thus far. After the third question I decided to take a breath. I told myself that since I had never missed a class, and although I may not have the enormous confidence I was accustomed to having while taking exams, I had to know the answers. After reading each question I stopped for a few seconds and waited for my thoughts to guide me to the answer. I let my reflex responses show the way. Within a few seconds my mind would fill with my answer. It was a short-answer essay exam. (If the exam is multiple choice your confidence will not take as much of a beating because the correct answer is there; it just comes down to choosing it). Anyway, I did this with each question and left the exam vowing to never again take a test that I had not sufficiently prepared for. As I walked to my car, I told myself that I had failed the test and I was angry because I was now going to have to work that much harder to maintain an "A" average.

My professor finally placed the exam face down on my desk. For an instant I wanted to throw the test into the trash without even looking at it, but of course I couldn't actually do that. I flipped the paper over and could not believe my eyes. There it was, a big circled, and underlined "A!"

Although I was completely negative about my ability to successfully complete the test, I calmed myself after reading each question and let my mind quietly search for the answer. I was purposely not thinking negatively. I was using my, as-ever, trusty mind to find the answer within that positive kingdom that can live inside us (though it is often dormant). Just as those exam questions were inside of me, so are the steps you will need to achieve your hopes and dreams within you. Just look inside yourself to find everything you want and need.

Control your thoughts; negative thoughts produce negative results. How will _you_ handle the next situation you find yourself unprepared for? How will _you_ eliminate worry to begin living the life of your dreams? Hurry, write them here.

_____

_____

_____

_____

_____

_____

_____

Remember, you can have anything you want. How you achieve this depends greatly on how much you believe it—how much you believe you can have _anything_ you want!

Introspection is the most difficult part of this process. It is where you will find exactly what you want. Sometimes really understanding what you want can cause you to think about why you don't already have it. Some of you will find that dealing with the challenges that come with achieving your goals are so uncomfortable that you give up your dreams and begin instead to turn on yourself. These problems are created by you so they can be solved by you through the positive power of your thoughts and the positive actions you take.

Join the conversation #pocket5worry

To hate and to fear is to be psychologically ill.

It is, in fact, the consuming illness of our time.

H.A. Overstreet
Social Psychologist

Hate is to have a strong dislike or ill will for.

At this age you will have very strong dislikes, and in many instances, these strong dislikes are OK. I hate lima beans, and I am probably the only person on the planet who did not like *The Lord of the Rings* trilogy. Hating foods or certain kinds of clothing or a particular movie is not detrimental to your well-being. It is when you have strong dislikes for others or yourself that you get into trouble. Having a strong dislike for someone only hurts you. Spending your time and energy thinking about people you dislike is a waste of time and creates negative emotions inside of you. This is when the negative "kingdom inside" gains strength. The reason to dislike someone and to continue to THINK about them is to experience an irrational form of pleasure. Due to deep-seated emotional challenges it is easy to find enjoyment in ruminating on negative thoughts about someone. You begin to enjoy your hatred. It somehow does not quite feel like a negative emotion because you play out in your mind the various ways to find revenge and the idea of taking revenge gives you pleasure.

Jack Canfield, the coauthor of the "Chicken Soup for the Soul" series, states in his book entitled, *The Success Principles:*

"All people (including you) are always doing the best they can to meet their basic needs with the current awareness, knowledge, skills, and tools they have at the time. If they could have done better, they would have done better. As they develop more awareness of how their behavior affects others, as they learn more effective and less harmful ways to meet their needs, they will behave in less harmful ways."

People do the best they can with what they have at any given time. You are doing the best you can with what you have at this time. This book will help you improve as a person by developing your awareness, knowledge, skills, and tools. Of course, there will be people you dislike, but you must not indulge yourself by spending time thinking about them. If you dislike someone, or something, simply acknowledge that fact and move on. Never spend more time with them than needed. Refuse to spend time thinking about how much you hate them. Thinking about them enables them to steal your future from you. Why give them more opportunity to hurt you? Thinking about people you dislike allows them to continue to harm you simply by spending time thinking about them; not thinking about *your* future life (*without them*).

For many years I thought I hated my father. His constant drinking, gambling, and womanizing were a major part of the problems in my family. From a small child, until I left home, there were many nights when I was awakened by the sound of my parents arguing. This was an ongoing process; a terrible habit. I now know that they were doing the best they could under the then-current circumstances. I interpreted my father's drinking as a lack of love for us; that we were so intolerable that he had to drink to be able to stand his current situation. I don't know why my father never decided to get sober. That is something I will never know.

About the time I was 25, I finally stopped asking why. I was an adult and needed to get on with my life. He had chosen his life, and there was nothing I could do about it. Do I THINK I would have become a complete person sooner had my father been sober? Perhaps, but that is insignificant because I am continuing to move forward with my life and without that experience I may not have fully understood how detrimental hate can be. Be careful, because the negative side of "life" can get the best of you. Do not wait until you're 25 years old. Give up the feeling of hate and begin creating a peaceful inner kingdom.

THINK about the people you intensely dislike then replace that thought with something positive like "I only use my energy to THINK about my future goals." Also, each time one of these individuals creeps into your mind, immediately repeat the statement; "I only use my energy to THINK about my future goals," or you can simply tell yourself to "cancel that thought." Write I only use my energy to THINK about my future goals 15 times.

_____

_____

_____

_____

_____

_____

_____

_____

_____

_____

_____

_____

_____

_____

Join the conversation #pocket5hate

Resentment is like drinking poison
and then hoping it will kill your enemies.

Nelson Mandela
Winner of the Noble Peace Prize

Shame is a painful sense of having done something wrong; feeling disgrace and dishonor. (Guilt, on the other hand, is a feeling of responsibility for wrong-doing.)

There is no shame in not knowing;

the shame lies in not finding out.

Russian Proverb

As a result of your parents trying to teach social graces shame is felt from a very young age. Have you ever felt that you had done something wrong when you really had not? This is the result of past unresolved ridicule emanating from yourself and the ridicule of others that you believed to be true, some of it coming from childhood. Often you may find yourself ashamed of your siblings, or your parents, or something your best friend did. Shame is a subtle form of self-hatred. You feel ashamed of your little brother because he always "shows off" when your friends are visiting. You feel ashamed of where you live, because the neighborhood is too poor, or too rich. Why should you feel as if you have done something wrong when your little brother or sister is misbehaving? Why should you feel you have done something wrong when it was your parents who decided where it is that you live? Feeling ashamed is what I call an extension feeling. It is the extension of your brother's or parent's behavior that has caused you to feel a particular emotion. Shame is a severe form of self-abuse. Take care of yourself by not feeling badly about anything, especially anything that someone else has done.

THINK about what is currently causing shame in your life and write each one down. Write what you will say to yourself to move away from this negative feeling. How will you handle shame the next time you feel it?

_____

_____

_____

_____

_____

_____

_____

_____

_____

_____

_____

Join the conversation #pocket5shame

In darkness one may be ashamed of what one does,

without the shame of disgrace.

Sophocles
One of classical Athens' three great
tragedy playwrights

Guilt is a feeling of responsibility for wrong-doing.

Guilt is the source of sorrow, 'tis the fiend,

Th' avenging fiend, that follows us behind,

With whips and stings.

Nicholas Rowe
English dramatist who was selected
Poet Laureate in 1715

Guilt is the feeling of being responsible for something wrong. It is not as painful as shame. When you feel shame you THINK the feeling is justified because the shame is often the result of someone else's actions, but guilt can be equally damaging. Guilt is often a product of your own doing. You yelled at your mother and now you feel terrible about it. You do not want to attend a friend's party and you feel guilty. Guilt does have a measure of goodness. It helps you to keep your word and follow through when others are depending on you, but feeling guilty all the time or for no apparent reason or as a result of trying to please someone else, that is what causes troubles. Guilt helps you to stay on track with your life, but it is only helpful in small doses. Refuse to overdose on guilt or you will find yourself paralyzed by it. When you feel guilty take a moment and THINK about what is happening. THINK about your feelings, make the appropriate adjustment to your actions, and move on quickly.

THINK about some of the things you currently feel guilty about and write them down. Analyze the irrational feelings you have about each situation. Replace these feelings with a more positive outlook and decide, right now, to let go of the guilt.

_____

_____

_____

_____

_____

_____

_____

_____

_____

_____

_____

_____

_____

_____

Join the conversation #pocket5guilt

Guilt is anger directed at ourselves.

Peter McWilliams
Author of You Can't Afford the Luxury of a Negative Thought

POCKET #6

Anger

(The Queen)

#pocket6anger

Whatever is begun in anger ends in shame.

Benjamin Franklin
American Statesman

Anger is a feeling that may result from injury, mistreatment, opposition, etc.; it shows itself in a desire to hit out at something or someone else; a strong feeling of displeasure.

You are probably never told to not feel anger, but are always told not to be afraid. Although anger is a negative emotion, it warrants a separate pocket because of its volatile nature. It is as natural as breathing, but can often be difficult to control. Anger is our comfort place, our home. It is the center of all of our negative emotions. As a result of anger you can find complete anarchy inside of you. The Queen, Anger, along with the King, Fear, can combine to create an inner kingdom that can decimate your outer world. It is often fear that stops us from doing things, and it is anger that opens the flood gates and allows you to lose control.

Many of you fear how you may react to a situation and decide to avoid social activities. You may attend a party and find that no one will sit next to you, let alone talk to you. Many people experience this form of isolation, but what they fail to realize is that it is they who have isolated themselves. Fear petrifies into a boulder that gets in front of you, holding you back and keeping others away. Get up, walk over to a group of people and introduce yourself. Call that person and ask for help. You will find that most people are so impressed by this that they instantly THINK that you are overflowing with confidence and not feeling what they, themselves, may also be feeling, a simmering of negative emotion.

This simmering, headed to an emotional boil is very destructive. Many of you are constantly at a simmer. This constant underlying feeling of fear and anger can become so commonplace that you no longer recognize them as being very negative and destructive emotions. They just sit there, hiding in plain sight, creating a generally miserable disposition for you. Although you may smile and appear to be relatively pleasant but if someone bumps into you or gets in front of you in line anger appears instantly. When faced with even a small amount of stress, the anger rushes to full boil like a football player who tackles your positive thinking, leaving everyone around you like a sacked quarterback, shaken and dismayed—at you! Fight the temptation to boil over with anger. Turn the heat off under your negative thoughts and cool the simmer. Anger is a human emotion and is a part of life. Just don't let it devour your dreams and ultimately your future.

List the things, the circumstances, or the people you currently feel anger toward and beside each item write why you are angry. Look at the list and decide, right now, to resolve these issues. It may involve confronting a person, eliminating them from your life, or, ultimately, forgiving them. Choose one of these three things, do it, and then move on. THINK about how anger is robbing you of energy that should be directed toward your future goals and your current happiness.

_____

_____

_____

_____

_____

_____

_____

_____

_____

_____

_____

Epileptics know by signs when attacks are imminent

and take precautions accordingly; we must do the same in regard to anger.

Seneca
Roman philosopher
Mid-1st Century AD

Recognize the feeling of anger and change your thinking. Wherever your mind goes, your body will follow. How will you handle anger? List your solutions here.

_____

_____

_____

_____

_____

_____

_____

_____

_____

_____

_____

_____

_____

_____

_____

Anger, that very strong feeling of displeasure, is a most fascinating feeling. You can turn it inward, toward yourself, or outward, directed at others; or both. How should anger be managed? Like the beast it is. It must be heavily chained in the recesses of your emotions and never allowed to get out of control. When displayed at inappropriate times, anger is one of our most destructive feelings. There are rare occasions when a display of anger is warranted, but never let anger consume you. Guard your inner kingdom from the Queen, Anger, for she has the ambition of Lady Macbeth.

Join the conversation #pocket6anger

Anger will never disappear so long as

thoughts of resentment are cherished in the mind.

Anger will disappear just as soon as thoughts of resentment are forgotten.

Buddha

POCKET #7

Whatever

#pocket7whatever

Whatever you hold in your mind will tend to occur in your life.

If you continue to believe as you have always believed,

you will continue to act as you have always acted.

If you continue to act as you have always acted,

you will continue to get what you have always gotten.

If you want different results in your life or your work,

all you have to do is change your mind.

Unknown

Whatever means of any kind at all; of no matter.

Are you part of the *whatever* generation? Do you no longer have an opinion and answer, *whatever*, to most questions? Do you have a lack of emotion—the opposite of fear and anger? Answering with *whatever* is a sign of apathy. Are you really indifferent about your life? Are you already convinced that *whatever* you do, it will not matter? Be an active participant in your life. Never let circumstances, friends or family determine what you do with your life. Refuse to let anyone discourage you. Do not let their *whatever*, (their apathy), discourage you. When you are angry you're much more likely to say *whatever*. When you feel fear, worry, hate, guilt and shame, you're more likely to say *whatever*. Stop pretending you do not care about a situation. State your feelings without saying *whatever*.

Refrain from being a bumper car in life. You are the boss of your life. You decide what thoughts, images, feelings, and actions to take. Be an active part of life. Tell people what you THINK. Tell yourself that you can do *any-thing*. The next time temptation overwhelms you to the point of saying, *whatever*, THINK about how you really feel and say *that!* Be an important part of the world. Never let *whatever* consume your life. Remember, you can have, do, or be, **whatever** you want!

What will you do the next time *whatever* enters your life? List your solutions here:

_____

_____

_____

_____

_____

_____

_____

_____

_____

_____

_____

_____

Join the conversation #pocket7whatever

Time is one of the essential ingredients.

Each day brings 86,400 seconds.

Whatever isn't used is gone forever.

Unknown

POCKET #8

Humiliation/ Embarrassment

#pocket8humiliation/embarrassment

The basis of shame is not some personal mistake of ours,

but the ignominy,

the humiliation we feel that we must be

what we are without any choice in the matter,

and that this humiliation is seen by everyone.

Milan Kundera
Czech Novelist, Playwright, and Poet

Humiliation is to lower the pride or dignity of oneself or another, or is the result of having done that.

Embarrassment is to cause oneself or another to feel ill at ease, or is the result of having done that.

Humiliation is a feeling most teenagers seek to avoid. You will attempt to avoid it each day. Appearing foolish causes hurt feelings and an enormous amount of shame. Teach yourself to move quickly from humiliation to humility; from a lowering of your pride or dignity, to a state of quality of your being in both mind and spirit.

I was regularly in a state of humiliation when my father came stumbling home from his work as a fireman, completely drunk. I remember thinking that everyone in my neighborhood thought I had a terrible life. Never mind that worse things were actually happening to many of my neighbors; all I was aware of was that my father walked home from the neighborhood firehouse and everyone saw him drunk—every day! He would often fall asleep on the front steps and a neighbor would have to ring the doorbell so we could help him inside. Of course, *I* was the one who answered the door, completely humiliated.

Another example of similar humiliation was when friends from school visited. I was completely occupied with anxiety the whole time they were there, because I knew my father would return home at any moment, drunk. Just as I had feared, he did get home before my friend and her boyfriend had left. He performed his usual antics: cursing, yelling, and saying awful things. I was so embarrassed that I ran upstairs to my room, sobbing uncontrollably. My friend and her boyfriend followed to console me, telling me not to worry about what had just happened. They *both* said that their fathers behaved the very same way. We wound up laughing hysterically as we discovered that their fathers were much worse. As I THINK more about this, I continue to find it humorous. I know now that no one really cared. However, while I was a middle and high school student I had not yet come to realize that most people are involved with and thinking about *only* themselves. What we fear we suffer alone is suffered by many. Know that everyone has humiliating challenges and struggle in the same way.

There was another humiliation I endured while in middle school gym class. After each gym class we were required to shower. At that age I was so self-conscious about my body it was absolutely agonizing to take a shower publicly. The only way to avoid this was when you were having your period. This was actually even more humiliating than taking a shower with my classmates. To avoid taking a shower you had to show the gym teacher your bloody sanitary napkin. As a middle student, I did not know that one could object to this kind of invasion of privacy. (Actually, that solution was not something that was available to one in that period of our country's history. We had not yet become aware of personal rights.) It never occurred to me to complain because complaining would suggest that I did not like showering. Adults had created this rule so I assumed it was an appropriate rule. Not until I became an adult did I realize that it was not appropriate.

It was a doubly humiliating rule because girls in middle school are likely to have just begun their menstrual cycles and are consumed with embarrassment about the whole thing. If anything like this is happening to you, tell someone. It is important to stand up to fight against what is humiliating. Adults can create rules that are not only humiliating, but are sometimes dangerous and illegal.

What are some of your most humiliating experiences? Write them here with your solutions. How will you fight the negative feelings associated with that humiliation? Tell someone immediately if you find yourself in a situation that just does not seem right.

_____

_____

_____

_____

_____

_____

_____

_____

_____

_____

_____

_____

_____

_____

_____

Join the conversation #pocket8humiliation/embarrassment

In a humble state, you learn better.

I can't find anything else very exciting about humility,

but at least there's that.

John Dooner
Chairman and CEO of Interpublic,
the world's largest advertising conglomerate

POCKET #9

Money

#pocket9money

Too many of us look upon Americans as dollar chasers.

This is a cruel libel, even if it is reiterated thoughtlessly by Americans themselves.

Albert Einstein
1879–1955

Money is any coin or paper stamped by government authority that is used as a medium of exchange and is a measure of value.

Money is the powerful, and often elusive, tool associated with success. Success is often measured by how much money you have. Everyone wants more of everything, but it is taboo to want more money. This societal tool is a contradiction. Secretly we want and need more money, but publicly we pretend that we have plenty of it. Acting *"as if"* is a step in the process of gaining wealth, but in most cases many pretend that they have more money than they actually have out of the fear that someone will discover their financial inadequacies; and those who *do* have wealth often pretend that their financial condition is less; more like people of average means (the shame of having too much). Your feeling of financial adequacy or inadequacy will likely come from your parents. They are feelings that have been, and continue to be, instilled during childhood.

It is important to have a healthy view of money. One's emotional attachment to money must be positive, because money is a useful tool for doing *good* in the world. Negative emotions about money, such as guilt, greed, or envy, are the real roots of evil.

I remember talking to a classmate when I was in the second grade and she told me how she practiced piano each day after school. I began thinking that I would love to learn such a wonderful skill. I rushed home and asked my mom if I could take piano lessons. She told me that we could not afford it, but, even at that young age, I recognized that there was an emotional element in her denial. She gave me that "look" as though piano lessons were not a part of our world; that such an activity was beyond our social standing as well as being completely outside of our financial ability. It was a look you'd recognize. It was a look that was disappointing to me; a sign that wanting "more" might even be something evil. What exactly my mother was really thinking I don't know. My interpretation was from the point of view of a child so this may not accurately convey what she was really thinking.

That was the beginning of my feeling that my hopes and dreams were alien—the sort of hopes and dreams that weirdoes THINK about. My desire to take piano lessons denoted the beginning of having many unusual desires so far as my surrounding environment was concerned. These desires ranged from wanting to go to a wonderful public high school across town, to attending a prestigious college, to taking riding lessons, and later, to having my daughter attend boarding school. The alienation to this concept instilled during my childhood, continues to linger in the air to this day, but I have overcome it because of my desire to move forward educationally, socially, and financially. The look on my mother's face is not something unique to my family, society often offers the same look. Friends, family members, teachers, school counselors and coaches will often unknowingly have the same look on their faces when you tell them your plans. This look often represents their inner fears. You do not have to incorporate their fears into your life.

Wallace Wattles wrote nearly one hundred years ago *"the person who does not desire to live more abundantly is abnormal, so the person who does not desire to have enough money to buy all he (she) wants is abnormal."*

I eventually began to believe that wanting to have, do, and be, more than what our financial ability allowed, did not make me weird, it just meant that my hopes and dreams were different from my parents and often different from others around me.

A common theme among adults is, "I don't have any money and I worry about it all the time." What are your earliest memories of money? How do these memories contribute to your current view about money? Are your views positive or negative? List them here and then dissect each negative view to transform it into a positive one.

_____

_____

_____

_____

_____

_____

_____

_____

_____

_____

_____

Now **THINK** again. Are your thoughts and feelings about money the result of your earliest memory or have you already begun to **THINK** independently about money, adapting your feelings to your own positive thoughts as to how they relate to this powerful tool? List how they have changed.

_____

_____

_____

_____

_____

_____

_____

_____

_____

_____

_____

Do you want financial freedom? How much money do you want? How much money will you need to buy everything you want? How much money will you need to feel financially free? Write down your positive thoughts about money.

_____

_____

_____

_____

_____

_____

_____

_____

_____

_____

_____

_____

_____

_____

Many people have irrational emotions about money. They believe it is wrong (even evil) to be rich. They are frightened by a world of abundance, frightened of the enormous change that wealth will bring to their lives, and ashamed to want nice things. Being rich is neither curse nor virtue. It is a right that is listed in our Constitution—life, liberty, and the pursuit of happiness.

Having monetary abundance is a pursuit of happiness. Being rich does not involve only money; it incorporates all of the wonderful things and experiences you want to have during your life. If you have a desire to become rich, you have every right to pursue that desire even if your parents disagree, and even if you have your own conflicting emotions about it. Recognize your conflicting emotions as irrational and set out to accomplish your goal of becoming rich. Being financially independent is a goal just like getting a college degree. It is a positive decision for your future and you should apply equal effort and emotion to wanting to be rich and wanting to get a college degree. The emotion attached to these goals is both equal and good. Just as having a college education is good for you, so is being rich in all things; experiences, people, and money.

Join the conversation #pocket9money

There was a time when a fool and his money were soon parted,

but now it happens to everybody.

Adlai E. Stevenson
American Politician

POCKET #10

Dating

#pocket10dating

Remember that as a teenager you are at the last stage of your life

when you will be happy to hear that the phone is for you.

Fran Lebowitz
American Writer

A **date** is a social appointment with another person.

No matter what your parents say, dating is a nightmare for them. Even if you are dating little Johnny or little Suzie who has lived across the street from you since birth, they are anxious about your dating. Dating is not just dating. It is driving; it is access to money; it is potential sex; it is the possibility for drinking. Sex and drinking may not actually happen, but dating sets the stage for sex and drinking and is thus quite worrisome for your parents. Once you are in high school, keeping you from having sex and drinking and using drugs is foremost on their minds, so dating may be a challenge for you on the home front. Try to be reasonable about this. Go back to the three keys to a successful beginning discussed in the introduction: keep a clear mind (do not do drugs or drink alcohol), treat your body well (do not have sex while still in high school), and get A's and B's (do your best work in school).

Avoid having sex while still in high school. This is the "just say no" concept for sex. Instead of just saying no only to drugs, include just saying no to sex while you're in high school. I know, many of you are thinking, "how am I supposed to avoid having sex?" Even if you have already engaged in sexual activity, decide—right now—to stop. Here's how:

1. Don't be alone in the house (his, hers, or a friend's) with a member of the opposite sex, especially someone you find attractive. DON'T DO IT! This removes the opportunity to have sex.

2. Make it clear to the person you are dating that you will not have sex while in high school. Just about all your boyfriends and girlfriends will respect this because making such a statement is a sign of self-respect; once you have self-respect others will find it easy to respect you. Those who find it *un*acceptable are *not* worth your time.

3. Remember, sex means oral, anal, vaginal, or any sexual activity with your hands on another person. Do not make the mistake of believing that sex is only considered sex if it is done vaginally or without a condom. Oral sex, anal sex, vaginal sex, sex with a condom, sex without a condom, sex with your tongue, sex with your mouth, sex with your lips, or sex with your hands, elbows, or feet is SEX!

These are the tools for avoiding sex while in high school. You have too many goals and too bright a future to jeopardize it by having sex while still a high school student. Read *My Life in My Pocket for College Students* (when it becomes available) to see how to handle sex after high school. For now, avoid having sex while you are still a high school student. If someone insists on crossing the boundaries you have set for sex, drugs, smoking, and alcohol, then they are not good for you. Do not make excuses for these so-called friends. Terminate the relationship.

What will you do to avoid having sex while in high school? What will you say to the person who wants to cross the boundaries you have set? Write your ideas here:

_____

_____

_____

_____

_____

_____

_____

_____

_____

The Bad Boy/Girl Trap

Dating "bad boys" or "bad girls" may seem like fun, but it is a trap and tells the world exactly how you feel about yourself. The person you date is a mirror image of how you view yourself. If a person you date is a bad boy or girl it tells your family and friends that you have low self-esteem and want to be treated badly yourself. Being with a bad boy or girl may seem exciting because they usually are suave, cool, and the dreaded, "nice." Nice can have a negative connotation. It is often used as a metaphor for something that is not good and the word "but" often follows it in a sentence; for example, "He is nice and everything, but there's something about him that's just not right."

Dating a bad boy or girl is a form of cruel excitement; it demonstrates your underlying negative feelings about yourself desiring poor treatment. That desire can be very strong. You must stop and assess what this feeling really conveys to yourself and others. Is it something good about yourself, or is it the ugly side of yourself demanding to be fed?

Bad boys and bad girls are detrimental to your well-being. They rely on their good looks, popularity, apathy, and charm to win your attention. After you are lured in they take little bites out of your self-esteem; if you spend enough time with them they will eventually eat you completely.

How to Spot "Bad"

A bad boy or girl is generally revealed by the way they behave in the first five to ten minutes during which you talk to them. If they exhibit even the slightest bit of what you would deem unnecessary rudeness, creepiness or abruptness, refuse to give them the time of day. A bad boy or girl will:

- be rude to teachers.
- be rude to their friends.
- make snide remarks about other students.
- tease geeky students.
- tease people who are not like them.

- be unfriendly toward animals; not necessarily cruel, but a little unfriendly.

- always be late.

- be apathetic about school work and work in general.

Those are a few minor examples.

Some major indicators include:

- drug use

- criminal behavior

- not attending school

- not doing school work

- treating the opposite sex badly

- a complete hatred or dislike for their parents

- cruelty towards animals

- bullying

I had as a goal to only date an ambitious guy. Had this been my only goal I could be married to a jerk. A person with ambition and success would have attracted my attention, but my *Man Plan*, a list of the attributes a man would have to have for me to date him, included being kind and caring, sensitive, and he *had* to like women.

I THINK that plan saved me from a man who was extremely successful financially, but who exhibited very negative behavior. My list included grade point averages even though none of the men in my neighborhood went to college. The man I wanted to date would not spend his evenings at home rubbing the hair off the back of his neck sitting, watching TV in his Lazy Boy lounger. No one in a five-mile radius of where I lived met any of these qualifications; yet I met a wonderful man because I wrote down what I wanted and made very few compromises. Writing down what I wanted in a relationship helped to guide me to the person I wanted because my focus was clear. I could recognize my goal and move in directions that would put my goal within reach.

To view a copy of my "Man Plan" visit www.MyLifeinMyPocket.com and click on Book Series>HighSchool>Dating.

If you are currently in a bad boy/girl relationship, end it immediately and focus on establishing a happy, healthier friendship. What will you do the next time you are approached by such a person? Write down the things you will do and what you will say.

_____

_____

_____

_____

_____

_____

_____

_____

_____

_____

_____

_____

_____

_____

Join the conversation #pocket10dating

Watching your daughter being collected by her date feels

like handing over a million dollar Stradivarius to a gorilla.

Jim Bishop
American Writer

POCKET #11

Character

#pocket11character

Every good thought you THINK is contributing its share to the ultimate result of your life.

Grenville Kleiser
Author of inspirational books and guides to oratorical success

Character is an individual's pattern of behavior or personality; his or her moral constitution.

Deciding to avoid sex while attending high school will increase your self-respect. This decision will create a solid moral constitution. Your character is yours to create. Be impeccable in your behavior and with the way you speak, look, and THINK. Monitoring the way you speak, look, and THINK will guide you straight to success. This includes not only speaking with correct grammar and enunciating every syllable perfectly, it also relates to being true to the person you are and the person you ultimately want to become. Avoid conforming to the way people around you behave. Find an individual you admire and emulate that person. Eventually you will settle into the wonderful person you wish and are meant to be. Do the same for the way you dress and your general appearance. Choose your style but be neat and presentable. Russell Simmons built a huge business empire wearing Adidas sportswear. *What* you wear is not important. *How* you wear that clothing, *how* you speak, and *how* you THINK, that is the essential move toward success.

The "thinking" part of your character can be developed by the books you read or listen to; so, too, music. So long as the music you listen to brings with it a positive feeling, its type is not an important issue. It can range from Mozart to Kanye West or the Red Stick Ramblers. As long as you feel good while listening to it, it's good for you. Include among your CDs, or iPod listening, books that are biographies of people you admire and find fascinating—Abraham Lincoln, Sojourner Truth, Oprah Winfrey, Bill Gates, Steve Jobs and Simon Cowell are such fascinating people; there is an unlimited amount of information on success that you will find in biographies; their "secrets." Create a "Success University" in your CD or MP3 player by listening to biographies and books on success and you will be well ahead of your peers and many adults. Imagine how easily success will come when you reach adulthood if you spend 15 minutes a day listening to or reading these types of books. By the time you enter college you will be unstoppable and your character will astound even you.

Many colleges use the honor system. No one will watch over you during exams. Your character will act as your moral compass. The way to guide your moral compass is through reading and thinking correctly. Good character is a decision. You have to decide whether you are going to be a good person or a bad person or, more realistically, a pretty good person or a not so bad person. I recommend reading other books in this series as they become available.

Another way to build character is to always do more than is expected from you and, certainly, more than is required. Going the extra mile is not really a mile, it's more like going an extra inch (which requires only a tad more effort), and those daily inches quickly turn into miles and will crash you head-on into your goals.

The ultimate in character-building is to never quit when things become difficult. If you keep with a difficult activity, that activity will eventually become easier; as it flows from difficult to easy your character will develop in many positive ways.

Visit www.MyLifeinMyPocket.com and click on Book Series>HighSchool> Dating.

How will character affect your goals and your life? What type of behavior will you use to build that character? What difficulties are you presently facing that you will now decide to see through to the end? List them:

_____

_____

_____

_____

_____

_____

_____

_____

_____

_____

_____

_____

_____

_____

_____

_____

Join the conversation #pocket11character

It is the highest form of self-respect to admit our errors and mistakes and make amends for them. To make a mistake is only an error in judgment, but to adhere to it when it is discovered shows infirmity of character.

Dale E. Turner
Author of *Words of Wisdom*

POCKET #12

Boredom

#pocket12boredom

Boredom is hostility without enthusiasm.

Stewart Emery
Author of the international bestseller,
Success Built to Last

Boredom is a state resultant of a person or thing that wearies by being dull or uninteresting.

Boredom is a subtle form of negative thinking. One of the most common experiences among teenagers is the feeling of boredom. Tan Jin, in his introduction to *The Adventures of Alice in Wonderland*, describes boredom as "wanting something to want." Life seems uninteresting because you are not participating enough in the things you love. Concentrating your efforts on getting through high school and not taking enough time to THINK about your future or spending enough time doing the things you enjoy will cause boredom. To become a complete person you have to pursue a variety of interests. Stop boredom as it creeps into your life. At the very first sign of boredom read through your goals and plan do to something that moves you closer to that goal or find something that you love to do; it is a perfect storm if your goals include something you love.

What are the things you love, I mean *really* love? The things you love are evidence of your purpose in life. THINK carefully and list them. Then plan to do all of them before the end of the next 90 days. Post them on my blog at www.MyLifeInMyPocket.com >what's in your pocket and share with others why you enjoy a particular activity; share, as well, your future goals.

_____

_____

_____

_____

_____

_____

_____

_____

_____

_____

_____

_____

_____

_____

_____

_____

Look at the list. The things that you love are the things that make up the structure of who you are. The more you do things you love, the less you feel bored. If you love watching Internet porn or you love getting into fights, then your moral compass is off course. If you love to fight maybe you should try a Karate class; it worked for me. If you have inappropriate loves like porn, or fighting, or stealing, or lying, visit www.MyLifeinMyPocket. com and click on Book Series>HighSchool>Character.

If the things you love are genuine and are good for you, than you should pursue them with passion. Once your favorite things are recognized as an important part of who you are, you can begin to accept them for the good they will bring into your life. Accepting the things you love and doing the things you love leaves no room for boredom. Should you find yourself bored come back to the list above and do one of the things you love to do. If, say, snowboarding is your love, and you are sitting in your bedroom, go onto the Internet and look up Shaun White, or snowboarding in general, and enjoy yourself virtually.

What will you do the next time you are bored? List the many things you might do right here:

_____

_____

_____

_____

_____

_____

_____

_____

_____

_____

_____

_____

_____

_____

_____

_____

_____

_____

Join the conversation #pocket12boredom

Boredom is like a pitiless zooming in on the epidermis of time.

Every instant is dilated and magnified like the pores of the face.

Charlotte Whitton
Former Mayor of Ottawa

POCKET #13

Friendship

#pocket13friendship

A friend to all is a friend to none.

Aristotle

A **Friend** is a person who one knows well and is fond of.

At this stage in your life, friends are everything. Making friends is one of the few choices you get to make all on your own. Your friends bring you so much joy that it is hard to imagine not having them in your life. Here is something you will find hard to believe: five years after high school you will have forgotten most of them! The time you spend with your high school friends are the seeds you plant for your future. The people you associate with now will have a huge impact on the success you realize in the future, even though you may not remember most of them later. Your choices, as they relate to friendship, should match with those things you want most in life, whatever they may be. The people you spend time with, although you may not believe this, have an enormous amount of influence on your future. You are creating an exchange of habits between you and them. Some habits are good; while others may be detrimental to your future.

Your friends should match your desires. If you want to get "A"s and "B"s then your friends should be the kinds of people who get "A"s and "B"s. If you want to give up smoking, drugs, and/or sex, then your friends should desire the same, both for you and for themselves. It's so easy to get caught up in how nice a person is, but your friends should not only be nice people, they should have similar goals and dreams making your attainment of those goals and dreams that much more likely to occur. The people in your life must bring more than "nice" to the relationship. "Nice" is simply the requirement needed for you to talk to them; helpful friends with a positive outlook are the friends you need.

Who are your current friends? Imagine what their future will be like. Do their future goals compliment the goals you have for your own future? List them here and discuss how they will be helpful to this end:

_____

_____

_____

_____

_____

_____

_____

_____

_____

_____

_____

_____

_____

_____

_____

_____

Join the conversation #pocket13friendship

Pay any price to stay in the presence of extraordinary people.

Mike Murdock
Author of The Leadership of Jesus

POCKET #14

Intuition

#pocket14intuition

The intellect has little to do on the road to discovery.

There comes a leap in consciousness,

call it intuition or what you will,

and the solution comes to you, and you don't know how or why.

Albert Einstein
Physicist and Nobel Laureate

Intuition is the immediate knowing or awareness of something without the conscious use of reasoning.

That "gut" instinct we all have from time to time is called intuition. Use this instinct to help guide you to the success you desire. Think of instances when you knew, in your gut, that you shouldn't do a particular thing, but you did it anyway. This is what creates regret. Limit regret by listening to and following the guidance of your intuition. When faced with a decision, be it immediate or for some future event, stop and THINK about how this will affect your future. It takes only a few seconds to THINK about it; it requires neither a huge amount of thought nor time. Mostly, if you just stop and listen to yourself, the answer will appear almost instantly. It is when you allow yourself to get caught up in the battle of back and forth decision-making that you temporarily lose your quick ability to make great decisions. When you are caught up in the moment of that decision, you are no longer thinking, you are responding by feeling. THINK and feel in conjunction with the moment. A gut response must immediately follow a thought, so keep those thoughts positive. That way a good feeling (gut response) will follow because according to the book, *The Secret*, good feelings are the fuel for success. Written by Rhonda Byrne, *The Secret* discusses in detail how good feelings cause us to attract good things into our lives. This is an excellent source and should be read by anyone interested in living the life of their dreams as it gives many examples of how to THINK correctly.

These "caught up" moments are generally positive experiences; it may be something as benign as staying too late at a party when you know you have a paper to work on—go with your gut and go home. Do stop and THINK about your initial reaction, though, you may ultimately decide to stay at the party. However, you will have been a conscious participant in that decision and be well aware of the future sacrifice you may have to make because of it—in the effect of your lack of sleep on the next day, and maybe not finishing the paper on time.

The Look on Your Parents' Faces

As a child it is common to absorb the look on a parent's face into the way you feel. This is part of building the foundations of intuition. Receiving a feeling from your environment is a part of intuition. Now that you are in high school it is time to move from allowing the way you feel to be the result of a direct response to what is happening around you. For the most part, that has served well, but as you get older, begin to choose the feelings of well-being and happiness over your parents' beliefs on such matters and the general responses of others who are around you. You must now rely on intuition, the positive world inside of you, to guide you to success. In unfamiliar circumstances and surroundings, stop and listen to your gut and allow your inner self to work for you. You will never fail yourself! When it comes to intuition, if you THINK, visualize, feel, write, and act, the five senses of success (as was stated in the introduction to this book), life will become easier. Although it may be inconvenient to write down what you want at any given moment, the other four steps can be accomplished rapidly and will lead to correct decisions.

I talked earlier about the look on my mother's face when I asked for piano lessons. The look on a parent's face helps to build (or not) one's self-esteem. Does your parent's face light up when you enter the room? Of course, but not every time, and that is perfectly normal. Parents deal with an enormous amount of stress, so try not to be too hard on those parents of yours. Do you see love and affection on their faces when they look at you? As youngsters (and even as adults) one is often unable to distinguish between an expression directed at you and one that is a reflection of that person's feeling at that moment—which often has nothing to do with you. But, because they are your parents, you will likely take everything they do as being personal and all about you.

Try to imagine that the world no longer revolves around you (the core belief of a child). The nuanced responses of your parents (and others) often have nothing to do with you and those that are actually focused upon you are filtered through that unreliable funnel that strains those responses through the strong emotional attachment you have to your parents. Practice to not let the negative aspects of these interactions infiltrate your self-esteem; and know, just for the sake of your own knowing it, that you are loved and cared for, no matter how you perceive the expressions on your parents' faces, and no matter how good or bad their parenting skills. Your parents love you and want the best for you, even if that does not always seem apparent. Remember what Jack Canfield said,

"All people (including you) are always doing the best they can to meet their basic needs with the current awareness, knowledge, skills, and tools they have at the time. If they could have done better, they would have done better. As they develop more awareness of how their behavior affects others, as they learn more effective and less harmful ways to meet their needs, they will behave in less harmful ways."

List as many as you can, of the occasions during which intuition has served you well. THINK of them often. They will help you to remember that it is you who are the greatest resource for yourself—if you will but listen to your intuition.

_____

_____

_____

_____

_____

_____

_____

_____

_____

_____

_____

_____

_____

_____

Join the conversation #pocket14intuition

All the resources we need are in the mind.

Theodore Roosevelt
26th president of the United States

POCKET #15

Regret

#pocket15regret

Regret for the things we did can be tempered by time;

it is regret for the things we did not do that is inconsolable.

Sydney Smith
English Clergyman and Essayist

Regret is to feel sorrow for.

You may or may not yet have accumulated a number of regrets. Regrets are an unnecessary part of life. Labeling an experience as regret is a major time-waster, for doing so destroys positive thoughts, replacing them with negative images that are played over and over in your mind. Labeling something as regretful is a way to hold onto disappointment. Unfavorable things will happen in life. Regret will help increase uncertainty, as it applies to what you want. The more vague you are about life the more regrets you create.

You create regret. It is not something that just happens—regrets are like bumps from bumper cars. *You're* steering. The things you choose to label regrets are merely the necessary experiences in life that help to guide you to your goals. If you take risks while moving toward your goals you will bump into things you do not wish to bump into. These are the "road blocks of life," nothing more. These road blocks are there with purpose. They are there to help you see more clearly your future accomplishments forming. Road blocks are clarifying experiences. They should not be labeled as regrets. You gain clarity from having to go over or around or through those road blocks. Far too often these necessary and minor occurrences (all road blocks are minor occurrences) turn into major regrets. Don't allow them to. Major regrets will infuse your DNA causing you to see them as a natural part of who you are. Avoid this negative form of osmosis. Allow yourself a few major mistakes in life and numerous minor ones. These mistakes are not regrets; they are evidence of the roadblocks on the path to eventual success.

By the time I reached high school, I began to understand that getting what you want in life requires only that you ask for it; (though asking for help is one of the hardest things for anyone to do). Most adults continue to struggle with this difficulty, so it is curious how I developed the courage to stand up to a teacher while I was still a teenager. It was during Home Economics class. I had been out ill and missed a quiz. When I got my report card there was an incomplete for Home Economics. I immediately went to the teacher and asked her why I received an incomplete. She said that I had missed a quiz. I was unaware that I had missed a test and insisted that she remove the incomplete and grade me on all the other work I had done.

This incomplete had caused me to not be included on the honor roll list posted in the school hallway. I was embarrassed to not be included when I should have been. The teacher said she could not alter my grade without giving me a zero for the quiz I missed. That would have drastically lowered my average to 70. Giving me an "incomplete" was a way to get my attention, not to allow me to take the test I had missed. I felt so helpless! That night, as I lay in bed, unable to sleep, I wanted desperately to solve this problem. I decided I would write a letter to the principal, Dr. Elizabeth Edmonds (she died a few weeks before this book was published) and lodge a complaint against my teacher. I wrote the letter and finally was able to get to sleep. The next day I went to the Dr. Edmonds office and put the letter in her box. By lunch time I began to lose my nerve and went back to the principal's office to retrieve the letter. As I removed it from the box, Dr. Edmonds came out of her office and saw me. She asked me why I was removing the letter and I told her that I had changed my mind. She insisted that I come into her office and explain myself. I reluctantly gave her the note and sat in total agony as she read it. After reading the letter she said, "I'll look into this. Everything will be alright." I could see that she was angry, but I wasn't sure whether the anger was directed toward me or at the way I had been treated. I left her office filled with uncertainty.

That evening the teacher actually called me at home to say that she would be more than happy to give me a make-up quiz! Her entire attitude toward me had changed. By the principal acting on my request and remedying this with my teacher, I learned a big lesson and gained an enormous amount of confidence. It was the best gift I had ever received. I aced the test and got a great grade. Dr. Elizabeth Edmonds taught me how to solve problems. I learned that when you have a problem do not follow your own self-imposed protocol by going to the person next in line; start with the person at the top. These are the individuals with the power to help you and they will respect your need to demonstrate to them what is right.

I have always remembered the way Dr. Edmonds reacted to my problem. It was one of the first times in my life that I felt like my needs were important. She taught me so much with that one act. Her actions helped me to love and care for myself. She taught me how to help those in need and to help them despite their reservations about needing help. But most of all she gave me courage, the courage to ask for what I want.

Ask for what you want and focus your full attention on the here and now and how it relates to your future and do not waste time with the past; good or bad it cannot be relived or changed. For years I regretted not having parents who expected me to attend college. They were not necessarily against it, but there was neither encouragement nor support. I was on my own. Paying application fees and completing the paperwork on my own was worrisome. All throughout my time in college I felt cheated by the lack of support by my parents. I kept thinking how much easier my academic life, and life in general, would be if I had some support. Such thoughts are a complete waste of energy. I now recognize that my parents were doing the best they could at the time. The good thing is, that as a result of the lack of this support I am now completely self-sufficient and believe that I can do just about anything; especially when others say I cannot, or display that 'look" on their faces either verbally or by demonstration of their apathy.

What regrets do you harbor? List them here. How will you neutralize these regrets and reroute your thinking in order to move forward with your hopes and dreams?

_____

_____

_____

_____

_____

_____

_____

_____

_____

_____

_____

_____

_____

_____

_____

Join the conversation #pocket15regret

"As you grow older,
you'll find the only things you regret
are the things you didn't do."

Zachary Scott
American Actor
1914–1965

POCKET #16

Conformity

#pocket16conformity

I learned much later to worship her,

just as I learned to delight in cleanliness,

knowing, even as I learned, that the change was

adjustment without improvement.

A conversation about Shirley Temple from the book

"The Bluest Eye"
By Toni Morrison

Conformity is action in accordance with rules and customs.

"Adjustment without improvement," Toni Morrison's words are so true. Conformity is adjustment without improvement. Initially your actions may mimic your parents or caregivers. You learn how to behave based on the manner your parents behave and in the manner in which you were treated. This is part of normal development; however, many will continue to mimic neighbors and the mores of society.

The Declaration of Independence states:

"We hold these truths to be self-evident, that all men [and women] are created equal, that they are endowed by their Creator with certain unalienable Rights that among these are Life, Liberty, and the pursuit of Happiness"

"Endowed by their Creator," suggests that simply by being born you have the right to Life, Liberty, and the pursuit of Happiness. It is your *duty* as a citizen of the United States to pursue your dreams. It is your *duty* as a human being to pursue your dreams. This country was founded on a dream and that enormous dream became reality. If man can dream of creating

83

what has become the most powerful country in the world certainly, then, whatever dreams you have for yourself will become a reality too!

It is important to be the individual you choose to be. Refuse to conform to what your friends or neighbors do. Be yourself. Be outstanding. Be courageous. Be kind. Be willing to learn new things. Be willing to THINK about things in a different way. Be creative with your thinking. THINK outside of the ordinary. Expand your mind and you will expand your life. THINK about what you want to be. Avoid limiting yourself by failing to limit your thoughts.

THINK **BIG**.

You can have, do, or be, anything! Do not fall into the trap of being like everyone else. Fail to make adjustments without improvement. Shakespeare said *"to be or not to be, that is the question."* It is one of the most important questions in life. Answer it BE!

What will you be? Decide RIGHT NOW! Write down what you will do with the rest of your life, what you will be, and how you will do it *your* way.

_____

_____

_____

_____

_____

_____

_____

_____

_____

_____

_____

_____

_____

_____

Join the conversation #pocket16conformity

Follow the path of the unsafe, independent thinker. Expose your ideas to the dangers of controversy. Speak your mind and fear less the label of "crackpot" than the stigma of conformity. And on issues that seem important to you, stand up and be counted at any cost.

Chauncey Depew
US Senator from New York
1899–1911

POCKET #17

Loss

#pocket17loss

Unhappy that I am, I cannot heave My heart into my mouth:
I love your majesty According to my bond; nor more nor less.

William Shakespeare
from King Lear

Loss is to be deprived of; not to have.

The loss of a friend is often so unexpected that it is devastating. There will come a time when you will lose a best friend. The two of you will have a disagreement that escalates, as many disagreements do, to a point where one or both of you will refuse to reconcile. It is devastating, but remember, life is filled with change. Change is the only thing that is a constant; your friends will likely change as time moves forward.

My best friend seemed so desperate during our parting conflict. I felt so sorry for her, and I—a writer—was at a loss for words. I wanted to help her, but I knew her emotions were raging at a level beyond my ability to calm them. I could feel her absolute contempt for me. The day of that disagreement I had just taught a class on conflict resolution at the local college. Smack in the middle of our argument she referred to me as "Ms. Conflict Resolution" suggesting that I really knew quite little about the subject. I knew, right there and then, that she held strong ill feeling toward me.

You will lose friends as you set and achieve goals. One of the hardest things in life is to get started and pursue to follow through. You can want something so badly for the people you love and care about but that will not motivate them to achieve.

We often hold ill feeling toward those we care about. This is not necessarily a bad thing. It is impossible to like everything about someone all of the time. However, this is when you can cause harm to a relationship and to those you care about in an effort to gain something over them; it can be devastating. It really hurts when you discover that your best friend holds contempt for you. I thought about the movie *The Count of Monte Cristo* wherein one of the two friends turns on the other causing him to go to prison. I was sent to a prison of isolation from my friend; the sentence, a result of her contempt. Sometimes friends are not really friends; even some "best" friends are not friends. This, however, is a normal part of life; every experience we have benefits us in some way.

Although the loss of a friend is awful, the loss of your hopes and dreams are exponentially worse. Giving up on your hopes and dreams is both a life-altering, and in many ways, a life-ending event. "Giving up" is very danger-ous to your happiness because it is a silent killer; you continue to hold your hopes and dreams in your mind, but you fail to take any action. When you only THINK about your hopes and dreams you can be lulled into a false sense of accomplishment; by being in a constant state of "getting ready" you falsely convince yourself that you are, in fact, working on your dreams. The reality of it is that you are just thinking about them—success requires happy, energetic action. Continually act on your ideas and avoid the quiet loss of your hopes and dreams through only thinking about them by add-ing physical energy to them.

There is a difference between interest and commitment.
When you're interested in doing something,
you do it only when it's convenient.

When you're committed to something,
you accept no excuses, only results.

Ken Blanchard
Coauthor of *The One Minute Manager*

The sting of doing work that others get credit for does not seem to lessen as you get older. When engaged in group projects do you feel it is likely to be you who will do all the work? Do not worry about this. Effort is a won-derful seed to plant. Do your best in all things even if it means you are the only one working. In any situation, according to Pareto's Principle, 20% of the people do 80% of the work. Always be one of the 20% and you will be justly rewarded financially as well as in your relationships.

Many people find it satisfying enough to just THINK and dream and talk about their great ideas without ever acting on them. Wonderful, glowing ideas are just ideas. Do not be fooled by those wonderful ideas and the positive feelings they produce, because without following through on those ideas they are nothing, just the fluff of your inner kingdom.

Do you have great ideas but have trouble taking the next step? Do not fall victim to such inaction. Take action in spite of those negative thoughts or the everyday busyness of life. There is always stuff vying for your attention. Do not let it get in the way. Make your dreams and goals your number one priority. Always do something every day; something that gets you closer to your goals. When that goal is reached set even bigger goals for your future.

How should conflicts with best friends be handled? What mistakes have you made when dealing with disagreement? What would you do differently? How will you handle the loss of a friend? Write them here as well as telling me your thoughts at www.MyLifeInMyPocket.com and click on Book Series>HighSchool>Loss. Also click on >What's in Your Pocket and Share Your Stories.

_____

_____

_____

_____

_____

_____

_____

_____

_____

_____

_____

_____

_____

Another Kind of Loss

Sadly, during high school, it is possible that you will experience the death of a classmate from illness or an automobile or other accident. It is an unfortunate reality and it is often the first time we experience death firsthand. During my high school time I remember two such deaths. The first was Jackie.

Jackie was the nicest person. She would get on the bus after me and we would often talk about school and about various teachers and students. We rarely spoke at school, so when she suddenly stopped getting on the bus I did not think much about it. It was several weeks later, when we neared Jackie's bus stop, that I asked a fellow student on the bus what had become of her. Another student answered by saying that she was the student who had killed herself a few weeks before. When we were told that a student had hung herself I did not connect the tragedy to Jackie. I felt so impotent. I felt guilty that I had failed to recognize that she needed help. I was heartbroken that I had not befriended her in the way she needed.

Jackie lived in a beautiful mansion in an old wealthy part of town. I lived in a row house in an impoverished part of town. In my immaturity I could not understand why someone living in a house like that could want to die. Looks are very deceiving. I continue to THINK about her often and as I write this I still feel like I should have been able to do something, but I also realize there is often nothing one can do. I will always remember her as a sweet, kind friend.

The second death that occurred while I was in high school was Carolyn. Carolyn was a beautiful young woman—bright, articulate, and sassy. I first got to know her in geometry class. After the first week of school I was finding geometry a bit challenging. I'm a "quick study," but geometry required a little more than I was accustomed to giving to a class. I noticed that Carolyn always knew the answers, so I asked her after class if she would help me. She gave me her telephone number and said that I should call her that night. We spent the next week, each night, after dinner, on the telephone going over the homework. She said the trick was to practice. Although math teachers often do not assign all of the problems from the textbook chapter, Carolyn did all the problems from each chapter anyway. I did this, too, just as she suggested, and found myself so far ahead of the class that I was left with more time to dedicate to my other subjects. This was a habit I extended to my other classes, and it served me well. You should try it, especially in classes you find difficult, or those in which you want to increase your grade. Carolyn not only taught me geometry, she made me a better student and helped me to build character by advising me to always do more than is required, and more than is expected. I will always remember how, after every quiz, she would turn to me to make sure my grade was an "A," and how proud she was to confirm that I had done well.

Carolyn died in a car accident in the spring before graduation and although our friendship never grew beyond her tutoring me during that one week, I often THINK of her and thank her for the wonderful lessons she taught me about geometry and life.

Have you lost a friend or relative through illness or an accident? Write their names and write a wonderful memory you have for each of them. Recall these wonderful memories often. Visit www.MyLifeIn-MyPocket.com and click on Book Series>HighSchool>Loss.

_____

_____

_____

_____

_____

_____

_____

_____

_____

_____

_____

Join the conversation #pocket17loss

Those who seek to achieve things should show no mercy.

Robert Greene
From the book, *The 48 Laws of Power*

POCKET #18

Vision

#pocket18vision

"The most pathetic person in the world is someone who has sight, but has no vision."

Helen Keller
American author and educator
who was both blind and deaf

Vision is the effect of and the power of imagination.

Visualize what it is that you want to have, be, or do—in Photoshop-pure colors! Imagine these things in their "full effect." Do not just THINK about the type of work you want to do, imagine yourself actually doing that work. Imagine sitting at the desk, standing at the podium, or being on the tennis court. Imagine how the room feels and smells or the warmth of the sun. View your vision from within the virtual reality of your mind's eye. Imagine it in 3D. Feel the wind blowing, feel the temperature of the room, feel the leather of the car seat, imagine the new car smell—and be sure to visualize what *you* want, not what others want, or what others want for you. Don't limit your imagination by only visualizing what you THINK you can get. Visualize what you want. Be generous with your imagination. Most people spend time thinking about what they do not want or limit their imagination to what they THINK they can get. Absolutely visualize what you want absolutely!

Create a Vision Board

A vision board is a poster with pictures of your dreams. It should include your favorite quotes and pictures of the house and car you want, as well as pictures of all the things you want for yourself and the people you care about.

The next page is a vision board. Begin adding pictures to it and then spend a few minutes each day looking at the board and imagining that you already have these items. Continue to add pictures. This is the way to manifest your hopes and dreams. You have to experience them mentally first. Visualization is a major part of the road to success. This is the second step in the five senses of success discussed in the introduction. Visualize everything from taking tests to having millions of dollars in your bank account. As stated in the movie, *Platoon*, "wherever your mind goes your [body] will follow."

"Hell begins on the day when God grants us a clear vision of all that we might have achieved, of all the gifts which we have wasted, of all that we might have done which we did not do"

Gian Carlo Menoitti
Italian-born American composer and librettist

To view my vision board, visit www.MyLifeInMyPocket.com and click on Book Series>HighSchool>Vision. and tell me what you THINK.

Also visit Twitter @MyLifeinMyPocke (do not include the letter "T" at the end. I wasn't clever enough)

as well as #MyLifeinMyPocket and swap suggestions with others as to achieving goals.

Don't wait! Create your vision board NOW!

Join the conversation #pocket18vision

My Vision Board

Include pictures of what you want to do as a career. Also include pictures of the type of house you want and the type of car you want to drive. If you want a plane include a picture of you in one or flying it.

My Vision Board

Include pictures of what you want to do as a career. Also include pictures of the type of house you want and the type of car you want to drive. If you want a plane include a picture of you in one or flying it.

My Vision Board

Include pictures of what you want to do as a career. Also include pictures of the type of house you want and the type of car you want to drive. If you want a plane include a picture of you in one or flying it.

My Vision Board

Include pictures of what you want to do as a career. Also include pictures of the type of house you want and the type of car you want to drive. If you want a plane include a picture of you in one or flying it.

POCKET #19

Sports

#pocket19sports

Every strike brings me closer to the next home run.

Babe Ruth
Baseball Player
One of the Greatest Hitters of all Time

A **sport** is an activity or experience that gives enjoyment or recreation.

Playing sports can be so exhilarating. My sport was Shotokan Karate. I did not find my sport until I was 24 years old because the high school I attended was more than a one-hour bus ride. I did not try out for a sport for fear that I would be unable to get home after practice. This was an irrational concern. I probably could have looked at the bus schedule and figured it out, but then how could I have gotten home from the games? My parents did not have a car, so I gave up the notion of joining a team. I also wanted to audition for the school play, but I had the same transportation concerns. Rehearsal was after school and the performance was on a weekend when the bus schedule was questionable. I gave up a lot because of my belief that I would not be able to get back home. I did not want to be stranded. Without money, I could easily find myself stranded far from home, I thought. I should have talked to the principal about this problem. I am sure that she would have helped me figure out a solution, but I didn't.

These days, my sport is tennis. I play tennis every day, as long as the court is not too wet. I love tennis because it is a mental as well as a physical sport. Tennis is all about belief, belief in the ability to dominate that yellow ball. Each time I step to the baseline to serve or return, I know I have to believe in my ability to control that ball and, just as I know I can control that yellow ball, I am equally confident in my ability to control my life. That is what playing a sport will do for you. If you have low self-esteem, the quickest way to build self-confidence is to play a sport. The confidence gained from physical activity converts into mental toughness. It is worth your time and your effort to participate in a sport.

As I said, playing a sport can be a wonderful experience. It will alleviate loneliness, fatigue, and it is a natural anti-depressant. The sense of belonging to a group provides camaraderie and is the easiest way to make friends. Acquiring a physical skill while participating in group competition increases self-esteem and it is a welcome relief from academics. Have you ever decided not to try out for a sport because of the fear of failure or some other irrational fear like the one I had? Never let fear stop you from experiencing new things, if you fail or are cut from the team so what? But, if this is something you enjoy doing, or have listed it as one of your goals, refuse to give up. Keep trying and you will succeed.

I have completely fallen in love with tennis. I began playing about a year ago and I have played nearly every day since. Tennis is quite similar to karate in that it is a battle of wills. It requires an enormous amount of mental stability and, surprisingly, calmness. Being overly excited or stressed can be detrimental to your ability to play tennis. I apply the same Five Senses of Success I instructed you to use to achieve other goals. I THINK, visualize, feel, write, and act when preparing for a tennis match. In fact, for each tennis stroke you should first visualize where you want the ball to land before actually hitting it. It is a magnificent way to practice visualization. I recently won my first tournament and was voted "best newcomer" at the country club.

Another form of recreation, although not a sport, is clubs. Clubs provide much the same benefit and are a great way to grow in a variety of areas. Clubs like chess, math, song-writing, photography, or anime can serve the same purpose as sports like soccer, fencing, basketball, or tennis. If you have an interest that is not represented in a group at your school, start one. Schools should also expand from the traditional club concept and implement new groups like ones interested in eliminating poverty, hunger, tutoring, or fundraising for those in need. Or, there are mastermind groups in which students help each other become successful. Sometimes these activities are organized as once-a-year occurrences, but imagine the great work you could accomplish by organizing a weekly club dedicated to an altruistic goal.

Visit www.MyLifeinMyPocket.com and click on Book Series>High School >Sports.

Always remember to ask of those who have the power to help you with your problems to help you. Successful people are always willing to help. Find the highest ranking person in the organization you wish to work with and send them a letter to ask for a meeting or to ask them to help you. When it comes to achievement, teachers love students who have goals. Talk to a teacher about your future goals and then ask for advice on how to stay confident and focused. Sometimes you may need a little more time to finish a report, or you have a problem with a friend, or need advice about how to join a sports team (when, say, your parents don't have a car). Ask as many people as required, and you will find some of them more than willing to assist you.

What sports or clubs are you interested in? What steps will you take to join or to create a sport or a special interest club at your school? List them here.

_____

_____

_____

_____

_____

_____

_____

_____

_____

Join the conversation #pocket19sports

If your ship doesn't come in, swim out to meet it.

Jonathan Winters
Grammy Award-winning comedian,
actor writer, artist

POCKET #20

Cliques

#pocket20cliques

"Every clique is a refuge for incompetence.

*It fosters corruption and disloyalty,
it begets cowardice, and consequently*

is a burden upon and a drawback to the progress of the country.

Its instincts and actions are those of the pack."

Madame Chiang Kai-Shek
Head of the Chinese Nationalist Government in exile in Taiwan,
Wife of Nationalist Dictator of China

A **Clique** is a small, excluding group of people.

The dreaded clique! Do you really want to associate with a given group of people because they appear to be popular or they are what society labels as "beautiful people?" When these groups create like-minded ideas and perceptions they foster an (us-versus-them) mentality. Such groups may serve some purpose (I'm not sure what) but recall that it is your job to discover your *individual* views and opinions. You need to be free of group-THINK.

Cliques often carry a negative connotation because of their inherent exclusionary practices. The standard structure is that they are intolerant of individuals who do not meet given criteria. Although they may be comforting if you are a member, they are often viewed as a body supporting the purpose of keeping a certain type of person out. Remember you are an individual who is unique and powerful. Do not waste time complaining about cliques. Simply limit your participation in them.

I have always loved fashion. My high school had a club called, "The Fashionettes." By the time I was a senior I had a boyfriend with a car so I joined the Fashionettes because I knew he would drive me to and from the events.

The moment I joined I realized that the group was a clique. I was immediately totally isolated. Someone had told the teacher in charge of the Fashionettes that I was a trouble maker. (This may have been due to my love for debating in class—which was often viewed as over the top.) Anyway, when I joined, the teacher told me that she did not want any trouble and that I had better "watch myself." I found this perplexing but by this time I was not easily intimidated, so I continued with the group and did model in one of the Fashion Shows. I eventually left the club. Although they had warmed up to me a bit, they were not a very welcoming group of students. That said never let circumstances stop you from doing something. What I should have done was to form another club that had fashion as its theme or asked this teacher why she had formed such a negative opinion of me when we had never interacted.

Join a sport or club that you are interested in even if the members are not students you would normally spend time with. Meeting new people and taking risks is a big part of success. Cliques are often troublesome and, if you do choose to belong to one, maintain your individuality and confront all behavior that seeks to limit the participation of others. Be you! Be smart! THINK for yourself!

What will you do and what do you THINK about cliques? Will you let a clique keep you from joining a group that you are interested in? Will you confront the exclusive nature of cliques? Write your feelings below.

_____

_____

_____

_____

_____

Join the conversation #pocket20cliques

The worst cliques are those which consist of one man.

George Bernard Shaw
1925 Nobel Prize for Literature

POCKET #21

Feelings

#pocket21feelings

You have no idea what a poor opinion I have of myself

and how little I deserve it.

W.S. Gilbert
English Dramatist and Poet
1836–1911

A **Feeling** is an emotion.

Feelings are a good indicator of what you are thinking. If you are thinking negatively or having bad thoughts then you are feeling negatively or badly. Conversely, if you are thinking positively or having good thoughts then you are feeling positive or well. This dance between your thoughts and feelings is the precursor to becoming aware of what you are *actually* thinking and feeling.

It is very easy to move through the day without giving much attention to your thoughts and feelings. Bad habits set in by letting your negative thoughts and feelings flow freely. Awareness of these thoughts is essential to guiding your path to success. Once aware of your thoughts you can evaluate your daily activities, your positive thoughts and feelings, by differentiating between those feelings that are good and those that are bad. When you find yourself feeling bad, stop to assess your thoughts. Ask yourself, "What am I doing?" Then say to yourself "I need to THINK about _____ (fill in one of your goals) instead of feeling bad and go on to focus your thoughts on your current goal. When thinking about something unpleasant find the lesson in the gloom.

There is something positive in every negative experience and finding it will negate negative thoughts. Begin searching for the positive in each negative experience. This search for the positive is an excellent exercise for it causes you to THINK and to discover the benefits of the experience. Exercising your thought processes will cause you to actively seek the positive in any situation.

The next time you find yourself feeling bad how will you change your thinking? Remember, good feelings convert into the energy needed to take action; the energy needed to succeed. When thinking negatively, calmly move your thoughts to one of your goals. Do not have negative thoughts about your negative thoughts. List your remedies below:

_____

_____

_____

_____

_____

_____

_____

_____

_____

_____

_____

_____

Join the conversation #pocket21feelings

How many cares one loses when one decides

not to be something but to be someone.

Coco Gabrielle Chanel
French Fashion Designer

POCKET #22

Gratitude

#pocket22gratitude

There is more hunger for love and appreciation
in this world than for bread.

Mother Teresa
Winner of the Nobel Peace Prize

Gratitude is thankfulness.

Often, negative thinking and feeling bad is the result of a lack of gratitude. Just as there is always something wrong, there is always something to be thankful for. If you can always find something wrong, then you can always find something right and the something right is the thing to be grateful for. While in high school I almost never felt gratitude. I was so busy trying to do well in school that, outside of academics, I rarely thought about the good happening in my life. There was so much wrong on a daily basis that it took a tremendous amount of clarity to see the good, a complete clarity that has finally come through while writing this book. When I think of how Carolyn helped me with geometry and how my high school principal, Dr. Elizabeth Edmonds, helped me with a teacher I was having a problem with, I see the beauty of people in the world. There is plenty of good, as there always is: a beautiful sunny day, a helpful neighbor, the wonderful way your mother will make your favorite food without you having to ask for it, breathing, seeing, touching, hearing, smelling, and tasting; all are good things to be thankful for.

When I first began keeping a gratitude journal it took me several days to THINK of a thing to be grateful for and the one thing I could come up with to grateful for, was having a pen to write with. Sometimes you may find yourself so hopeless, so negative, so disappointed, and so full of fear, that it becomes difficult to THINK of even one thing to be grateful for. Gratitude can always be found in your ability to THINK, and thinking, parlayed with feeling and taking action, will solve any problem. Be grateful for thinking. Thinking is that part of you that has tremendous value, and when done correctly, will take you from an idea to a full blown three-dimensional tangible reality while you watch your, as the author Mike Dooley states, thoughts turn into things.

Start a gratitude journal right now. List everything you are grateful for (use a pad if you need more room ☺):

_____

_____

_____

_____

_____

_____

_____

_____

_____

_____

_____

_____

_____

_____

_____

_____

_____

_____

_____

_____

_____

_____

_____

_____

_____

_____

_____

_____

_____

Look at the bad things happening in your life and find something good in each one of them. It's all good! What's good today? (You shouldn't need a pad for this one):

_____

_____

_____

_____

_____

_____

_____

_____

_____

_____

_____

_____

_____

_____

_____

_____

_____

_____

_____

_____

_____

_____

_____

_____

_____

_____

_____

_____

_____

_____

In your lifetime you will hope for, and desperately need, a miracle; a miracle to take care of some devastating something. A **miracle** is an extraordinary event manifesting a supernatural work of God, the Universe or some other power. Miracles cannot be counted on; if they could, they would not be miracles. Several years ago, I remember watching an episode of Oprah. She was talking about how we should write in our journals five things each day that we are grateful for. This was during a very difficult time in my life and my journals were full of my troubles. I whined on and on about how miserable my life was. Writing about these troubles gave me some relief, but it was not a constructive use of my time.

Avoid writing about your troubles without including the solutions. Discover the gratitude you should find in those solutions. Always include gratitude in your daily thinking. Visit www.MyLifeInMyPocket.com and click on Book Series>HighSchool>Gratitude.

How will you maintain grateful thoughts and feelings? What are you grateful for today? Do you need a miracle? Begin a gratitude journal here:

_____

_____

_____

_____

_____

_____

_____

_____

_____

_____

_____

_____

_____

_____

_____

_____

_____

_____

_____

_____

_____

_____

_____

_____

_____

_____

_____

_____

_____

_____

_____

_____

_____

_____

_____

_____

_____

_____

_____

_____

_____

Join the conversation #pocket22gratitude

As we express our gratitude, we must never forget that the highest appreciation is not to utter words, but to live by them.

John F. Kennedy

POCKET #23

Action

#pocket23action

So many fail because they don't get started—they don't go.

They don't overcome inertia. They don't begin.

W. Clement Stone
Self-Made Multi-Millionaire

Action is the doing of something.

Positive action is fueled by your good feelings. To get where you want to be you must hold your dreams clearly in mind and be open to whatever ideas your mind produces, and then act on those ideas. There is no right way to achieve an end. Once your goals are set, things will just open up for you. A clear vision of your dreams will help you to see opportunity. Deep down you know you can achieve your goals, but you probably believe that the process is much like trying to boil the ocean. The ocean can be boiled, it is water, but it will take enormous energy and a lot of time (along with a very large pot). So, if the ocean can be boiled, certainly your dreams can come true—all without an enormous amount of energy or a lot of time.

Thoughts are powerful but they are not all-powerful. You cannot just THINK positively, you must do something. Act on your thoughts. Take the first step when you get an idea; never analyze an idea too much. The fact that the idea came to you is cause enough to follow through on it. If it is a positive thought, some measure of impulsiveness is needed to follow through. Refuse to worry about how to accomplish a thing, just keep thinking about your goals and dreams, and the correct actions will appear. Forget about worrying about appearing silly or unprepared. Your thoughts will guide you through your actions to any and every result you seek. The way to keep your dreams and goals in the front of your mind is to keep them in front of your eyes. Write your goals down. Read them four times a day.

Quickly create a five-year plan. Without much hesitation, write whatever you want to accomplish during the next five years. Refer to some
of the goals you wrote about earlier. Remember, BE BOLD! Never allow the negative kingdom inside of you to censor your dreams; boldly
list whatever you want:

_____

_____

_____

_____

_____

_____

_____

_____

_____

_____

_____

_____

_____

_____

_____

_____

_____

_____

_____

_____

_____

Consult this list at least four times a day. Pick your top three goals and begin to THINK about them. Continually ask yourself, "How can I accomplish this?" Wait for the ideas to coalesce in your mind. Write them down and follow through on them with action.

One of your goals may be to get an "A" in history. Begin thinking of and visualizing that "A." Imagine all of your exams and quizzes coming back with an "A" at the top of every page. The action needed to accomplish this goal will appear in your mind and you can then follow through. Maybe you will need to call a classmate like I did in my story about Carolyn, or maybe you will need to spend an additional ten minutes studying the main points in your class notes each night.

The "trick" to getting good grades is simple. You must believe that you deserve good grades, attend class, pay attention in class, and reread your class notes from the day's lectures every night, if that is possible. It is unnecessary to study your notes, just reread them. If you do these things in addition to your assigned work, you will get fantastic grades. In fact, the amount of time needed to prepare for exams will be lessened. Also, when you feel confident that you know the material and have studied enough, continue for an additional ten minutes and you will undoubtedly be ready.

There is no right way or wrong way to achieve success. Just take the initial steps and your hopes and dreams will begin to take on a life of their own. Remember the Five Senses of Success, THINK, visualize, feel, write, and act. THINK about what you want, visualize it happening, feel good about it, write it down, and act on your ideas.

What will your life be like in five years? Where will you live? Where will you travel? How will you serve others? Write expansively:

_____

_____

_____

_____

_____

_____

_____

_____

_____

_____

_____

_____

_____

_____

_____

_____

_____

_____

_____

_____

_____

_____

_____

_____

_____

_____

What action will you take to begin moving toward the goals you have written in this book? Choose the single-most exciting goal and do whatever your inner self tells you do. Stop and listen to the guidance you give yourself. Do it and then achieve the next goal, and the next goal and the next. . . .

Join the conversation #pocket23action

POCKET #24

Begin

#pocket24begin

He who has begun has half done. Dare to be wise; begin!

Horace 65–8 B.C.

Begin means to be or do in the slightest way.

Begin where you are, right now! So many of you are so busy "getting ready to get ready," that you never begin anything. You have to escape the gravity of your own disbelief. The thrusters needed to move forward are found in action, not just in belief. Yes, believing is a large part of success, but if you are presently a little short on belief begin moving toward your goal by acting.

Action will negate belief. For example, smile a big smile and go on to do the action. I want a big, broad smile. While smiling, say loudly, "I hate my life!" It will be difficult to generate the negative emotion you need because the smile will get in its way. The action negates the feeling, so when belief escapes you, ACT! Act on your ideas in spite of what you believe. Take action. BEGIN!

In the movie, *Any Given Sunday,* Al Pacino talks about how getting "inches" in life relates to gaining inches in football. He states, "Some of you are in hell right now. You can stay where you are and get killed, (both literally and figuratively), or you can fight your way back into life."

Al Pacino goes on to say:

"Life's a game of inches. The margin for error is so small, a half step too late or too early and you're done. The inches we need are everywhere around us. You must fight for that inch; claw with your fingernails for that inch. 'Cause when you add up all those inches that makes the difference between winning and losing, between living and dying. Fighting and dying for inches is what living is and the guy willing to die will win that inch. Now, I can't make you

do it, but when you look in the mirror you will see a person who will go for that inch. **Now, what are you going to do?"**

You can render to God and humanity no greater service than to make the most of yourself.

Wallace Wattles
Author of *The Science of Getting Rich*

   To see how many times the word THINK was used in this book, first guess how often it appears, then visit www.MyLifeInMyPocket.com and click on Book Series>HighSchool>Thinking. Also include what you THINK about this book and tell me if *your* thinking has improved. Remember, as Earl Nightingale, author of *The Strangest Secret* states, "You become what you THINK about."

*You've heard the saying, "people get what they deserve."
Well, I THINK that people get what they THINK,
and what they THINK is what they deserve.*

Kathy L. Lewis
Author of the
"My Life in My Pocket," Book Series

Remember to use the Five Senses of Success: THINK, Visualize, Feel, Write, and Act to get any and every thing you want from life and then use the Sixth Sense of Success and repeat the steps. By repeating the steps you will gain full belief in your ability to succeed.

Join the conversation #pocket24begin

www.MyLifeinMyPocket.com

www.Facebook.com/MyLifeinMyPocket.com

Twitter @MyLifeinMyPocke
(do not include the letter "T" at the end. I wasn't clever enough)

#MyLifeinMyPocketHighSchool

 Kathy Lynn Lewis is a leading expert on Self-Advocacy. She has devoted the past fifteen years to helping families with children with special needs to advocate for their children, and now travels around the country speaking and leading seminars that help individuals and businesses achieve success through goal-setting and outlining, "what they want to have," "what they want to be," and "what they want to do." She is the President and Founder of The Ripple Effect (www.TheRippleEffect.tv), a company that helps businesses and individuals realize their potential by understanding what Earl Nightingale states, "we become what we THINK about," and that the impossible takes a little longer, *but not much.* Kathy is also the author of the *My Life in My Pocket* series of books (www.MyLifeinMyPocket.com). She lives with her husband and two daughters in Tampa, Florida.

Scan with any smartphone to learn more

CPSIA information can be obtained at www.ICGtesting.com
Printed in the USA
LVOW11s0828041113

359902LV00001B/7/P